DISABILITY
AND THE
DISPLACED
WORKER

DISABILITY AND THE DISPLACED WORKER

Edward H. Yelin

Rutgers University Press
New Brunswick, New Jersey

Library of Congress Cataloging-in Publication Data

Yelin, Edward H.
   Disability and the displaced worker / Edward H. Yelin.
     p. cm.
   Includes bibliographical references and index.
   ISBN 0-8135-1853-9 (cloth)
     1. Handicapped—Employment—United States. 2. Displaced workers—
United States. 3. Insurance, Disability—United States. 4. Age and
employment—United States. 5. Labor market—United States.
I. Title.
   HD7256.U5Y45   1992
   331.5′9′0973—dc20
                                        92-6863
                                         CIP

British Cataloging-in-Publication information available

Contents

List of Figures

List of Tables

Preface

Work disability had never been a central concern of the public or of policymakers until the dramatic increase in its prevalence in the 1970s and 1980s. Even then, we were not concerned about the problems persons with disabilities faced in work; we worried about work disability because we feared it was the leading edge of an aging boom that would render increasing proportions of the population infirm and hold the Federal budget hostage. We worried about it because wo feared that public policy was encouraging systematic malingering by providing a soft cushion of disability benefits. Thus, our work disability policies represent what I have called displaced concern: they are designed to deal with troublesome dynamics—aging, expanding entitlement—in which the employment of persons with disabilities plays only a part, albeit a visible and malleable one. Population aging and the expansion of entitlement are inherently controversial because they raise the specter of generational conflict, old and out of the labor force versus young and in it, as well as class conflict, those deriving their incomes from work or assets versus those deriving their incomes from public programs. Persons with disabilities fared poorly in both dynamics for two reasons. First, their principal source of income, the Social Security Disability Insurance (SSDI) program, paid far more than other public entitlements, making them a visible target for those claiming that welfare reduced the will to work. Secondly, in contrast to other entitlements granted on the basis of income or age, adjudicating disability claims is inherently a subjective process. Because entitlement criteria can vary, they did vary. Because disability entitlement can be cut, it was. In a cruel paradox, work disability was never a concern of the public until other problems became worrisome. At that point, tinkering with work disability came to be seen as the easiest way to deal with those other problems.

The purpose of this short volume is twofold: to show that work disability is not a sideshow to aging and health dynamics or to social welfare expenditures and to suggest that in making it so, we forgo an opportunity to design public policies to actually reduce the prevalence of the problem. Instead, work disability has its own dynamic, tied to the transformations occurring within work, both good and bad, that displace older workers, particularly older men with disabilities, from the labor market. I argue that the focus on vague or abstract social forces, such as aging waves and the myth of malingering, allows us to displace our concern from what really is ailing us—the failure of the economy to generate enough money to sustain the standard of living we once knew and had come to expect as a birthright. People with disabilities have been victimized by this displaced concern, seeing their incomes fall and their motivations attacked in the press, in academia, and in Washington. But they are able to fend off the attack themselves. My contribution is to show that the attack was and is misplaced, and to redirect our attention to an arena less abstract, but much more troubling—the world of the modern workplace.

The displaced concern about work disability, of course, may be the perfect reflection of the decade just ended during which we were quite willing to indict anyone—but especially those receiving public entitlements—rather than admit that a stagnant standard of living came from a stagnant approach to making and selling things around the world. Persons with disabilities bore a disproportionate share of the attack on the welfare state, in part because they are the only recipients of entitlement funds who can be tied—even remotely—to the problems in the U.S. economy. Just as the psychological process of displacement prevents individuals from coming to terms with their problems, the displaced concern about persons with disabilities prevents us from confronting our economic troubles and from helping to reduce the font of work disability. The attack on persons with disabilities gave them a smaller slice of a smaller pie. The problem is the size of the pie.

Acknowledgments

In writing this book, I received encouragement, ideas, and an occasional bailout from many individuals and several institutions. It is no longer fashionable to thank the federal government for anything. However, without more than a decade of steady support from the Multipurpose Arthritis Centers Program of the National Institute of Arthritis, Musculoskeletal, and Skin Diseases and, during the last five years, from a National Institute on Aging Research Career Development Award, I would never have had the opportunity to spend time on employment issues, a nonstarter in the traditional medical school environment. The Arthritis Center here at the University of California of San Francisco has been everything one could want in an academic environment, providing a fertile ground to let my thoughts run wild and a fence to rein them in when necessary. Other colleagues at UCSF were generous with their advice and support—I hope they see some of it here— particularly Mike Nevitt, Jon Showstack, Phil Lee, Paul Blanc, Dorothy Rice, Mitch LaPlante, Ruth Greenblatt, John Spencer, Roy Kriedeman, and Jim Calvert. In the many years I was codirector of the Robert Wood Johnson Clinical Scholars Program, I subjected the program faculty and fellows here and at Stanford to endless revisions of my ideas. In particular, I want to thank Hal Holman for providing a forum, an ear, and some very helpful feedback. Hal has been a longtime supporter as dissertation adviser, colleague, and friend. As an unformulated set of ideas took shape, several colleagues around the country took the time to give my work a helpful nudge. Richard Scotch, Deborah Lubeck, Lois Verbrugge, Bill Johnson, Irv Zola, Bill Koopman, Jane West, Sue Hughes, Ted Pincus, Ed Berkowitz, Bob Meenan, in particular, proved trusted advisors. Marlie Wasserman, my editor at Rutgers University Press, gave me more of what authors want—support and encouragement—and less of what they don't. However, I must give special mention to two others, one formerly and one presently at the Milbank Fund in New York. As longtime editor of the *Milbank Quarterly,* David Willis played a special role in my career, first sheparding my research, and then teaching me how to communicate my ideas beyond the handful of people using the same jargon. He is the model of what a journal editor should be. And Dan Fox, now president of the Milbank Fund, has proven to be the most valuable of friends, mostly by helping me sharpen my ideas, in part by introducing them to policymakers through the fund's visionary Americans with Disabilities Act Implementation Project. To all these people, thank you.

But to three colleagues I owe much more. Patti Katz lived this project with me for the past two years. Gently, firmly, she has cajoled better work from me. Many of the ideas herein are rightfully hers; I hope she will let me repay the favor in the years to come. Curt Henke and I have worked together for more than a decade and a half. Endlessly patient, endlessly generous with his time and ideas, Curt's wisdom shines through day by day. I know my work is much the better for it. The President is always jabbering about a vision thing. Wally Epstein had a vision almost two decades ago that social scientists and physicians working together could make life better for people with chronic disease. Now that Health Policy and Arthritis Centers are all over the globe, we need to remember that he had the idea, but more important, had the savvy to make it happen. He continues to make it happen, with his support, friendship, and, yes, cogent criticism. I am honored to be his colleague.

As is usual, I save the most important for last. My mother, Jeannette Yelin, felled at any early age, and my father, Gabriel Yelin, still alive but with severe dementia, taught me to love learning, but only so far as we could use that learning to make the world a better place. As I get older, I appreciate their values more and more. My wife, Abby Snay, and my children, Jenny and Benjamin, contributed to this book by providing love, encouragement, and respite. I hope now that I will have more time for all of them. Abby, I can never repay what I owe you, from the wisdom imparted by your years on the frontlines of employment issues as director of the Jewish Vocational Service here in San Francisco to your faith in me. This book is dedicated to you and to your work.

DISABILITY
AND THE
DISPLACED
WORKER

1

Overview

This book is about the rising rate of work disability. Most analysts either attribute this rise to demographic and medical factors—the aging of the population causes the disability rate to rise—or blame it on a reduced will to work, abetted by entitlement programs that make withdrawing from work possible, if not profitable. I argue here that the genesis of the work disability problem lies in work itself, on the macro level from our inability to sustain the demand for high-wage labor and on the micro level from our unwillingness to create the kind of working conditions that allow persons with disabilities to continue to work.

Work disability was once an issue academics shunned as too uncomplicated to be worthy of their attention, and to the extent they paid attention to it, they did so in cursory and at times confusing ways. Thus, the term *work disability* has three distinct meanings in the literature, each of which has quite different implications for policy. Work disability is variously defined as a limitation in one's ability to work, determined by either a physician's examination or self-report; as the receipt of disability compensation of some kind; or as a change in actual labor force participation associated with illness or injury (either a reduction of work time or cessation of employment). In this book, I use the term *work disability* only in the third sense: a change in labor force status.[1] I am interested in changing patterns of disease,

---

[1]This definition of work disability follows Nagi (1976) and Haber (1971) in distinguishing among disease (a pathological process affecting the body's

impairment, and activity limitation as they affect capacity to work, but when I use the term *work disability,* I refer only to the ultimate outcome in terms of employment.

History of the Work Disability Problem

Academics traditionally shunned the work disability problem because they believed it to be an inherently simple process—an individual contracts a chronic illness or suffers an injury and consequently stops working—and the rationales for and against disability insurance remained as compelling and unchanging as they had been since Bismarck outlined them in the mid-nineteenth century, or at least since the Progressive Era in the United States. Indeed, Germany initiated sickness insurance for lost wages in 1883, a policy followed by no fewer than twelve other European nations in the ensuing two decades. Likewise, the Progressives originally included insurance for lost wages in their campaign for social insurance in this country, but they were rebuffed when private disability insurors described the futility of attempts to limit compensation to pure medical criteria. The passage of a national work disability insurance program had to await the high-employment years of the 1950s.[2]

---

stasis), impairments (the effect of disease on physical performance), activity limitation (the effect of impairment in physical or mental performance on capacity to do one's activities), and disability (an actual change in activities). In turn, disability compensation is defined as the receipt of benefits contingent upon loss of employment and certification of impairment due to illness or injury. A good discussion of the nomenclature of disability studies may be found in Verbrugge (1990).

[2]Starr (1982) reviews the European origins of disability compensation programs, noting that Bismarck saw disability compensation as a crucial way to accommodate to the growing radicalism of the industrial workers but that business interests foresaw the problems in distinguishing work disability from unemployment due to general business conditions. Berkowitz (1987) recounts a similar debate prior to the passage of the original Social Security legislation in 1935, during the height of the Depression. Business interests succeeded in arguing that disability compensation was impossible to police in a time of high unemployment. Thus, it is not surprising that a national disability compensation program had to wait until the postwar expansion of the 1950s: only low unemployment could allay fears that disability insurance would serve to compensate the healthy unemployed. This did, finally, occur in 1954 with the passage of the Social Security Disability Insurance (SSDI)

But as the 1980s began, this issue took center stage in policy debates. Work disability came to prominence for several reasons. First, the simple explanation as to why someone stops working after onset of illness did not work. Many individuals with no apparent disease claim they can not work any more and, worse, succeed in getting disability benefits, whereas many with

---

program. Even so, passage was secured only by the device of initiating a very small-scale program and then expanding it. Thus, the 1954 SSDI legislation merely froze the Social Security retirement credits of the disabled until they reached age 62, after which they would receive their earned retirement benefits. In 1956, the program was expanded to pay actual disability compensation to persons over age 50; only in 1960 was the age limitation removed and a full disability insurance program in place. Although SSDI is the principal disability compensation program, other programs covering large number of individuals include Supplemental Security Income (SSI), administered by the Social Security Administration for the poor aged, blind, and disabled without the requisite work history for SSDI, workers' compensation for those injured on the job, and disabled veterans' compensation (Burkhauser and Haveman 1982).

The disability compensation programs differ in their eligibility criteria, but each has the same basic structure. Applicants must be out of work for several months (or at least receive less than several hundred dollars in work-related compensation during this period), and then must show that they have a medical condition that precludes work. Certain conditions automatically entitle someone to benefits; this is called "meeting the listings," that is, having one of the conditions listed as precluding work. If someone has another condition, he or she must prove impairment sufficient to preclude work in the national economy. Some conditions are not listed because they are too rare or because most cases are mild. If someone has such a condition, he or she will try to prove its equivalency to the conditions on the listings. If this cannot be done, a physician must assert that the impairment is severe enough to preclude sustained work. Employment history (and local economic conditions) are given secondary importance in adjudicating applications for benefits, but invariably such considerations enter the assessment as to whether the individual can work. Almost all the controversy surrounding disability compensation centers around conditions that do not meet the more stringent criteria of the listings. Not surprisingly, the proportion of applications for benefits meeting the listings varies over time, giving rise to the competing assertions that individuals use disability compensation to avoid working or to cushion bad economic conditions. The rules governing the application process for disability benefits are described in Berkowitz (1987, particularly chap. 3, "The Administration of the Social Security Disability Insurance"); the performance of the process is evaluated in Stone's *The Disabled State* (1984, particularly chap. 4, "Mechanisms for Restricting Access to the Disability Category").

apparently debilitating conditions nevertheless sustain employment.[3] Eligibility for work disability depends on medical certification of work capacity, but the evaluation of whether illness precludes work or simply excuses an unwillingness to persevere has proven to be a difficult muddle. Reflecting this difficulty, fashions in disability evaluation can and do change. And these changing fashions can be put to use: by the individual, who may try to pry benefits loose, and by the state, which may attempt to clamp down on expenditures. Work capacity is a flexible concept, disability entitlement is a flexible process, and this flexibility may be unique among major entitlement programs. Thus, disability benefits became the principal venue through individuals tried to cushion shocks in employment and income and through which the state tried to cushion the impact of rising expenditures and declining revenues.[4] To judge by the dynamics of the major disability benefit programs, the individual had the upper hand during the 1970s, the state gained control during the early 1980s, and since then there has been a stalemate.[5]

Second, everyone is at risk for disability, and most of us know

---

[3]Approximately 15 percent of persons with the most severe limitations in work capacity are currently working. In contrast, about 30 percent of those with the most minimal limitations in work capacity are out of the labor force (Lando, Cutler, and Gamber 1982).

[4]The flexibility inherent in disability evaluations was noted as early as the second decade of this century, when the initial proposals for disability compensation were made. However, the full ramifications of how this flexibility is used have been explored only in the past few years, principally through the work of the political scientist Deborah Stone (1984), who argued in her book, *The Disabled State* that the state, the firm, and the individual conjointly regulate the ebbs and flows in the labor market through the disability compensation process and that they can do this because medical conditions legitimate a set of behaviors that neither firms nor the state would be willing to condone on a more general basis.

[5]The number of disabled-worker beneficiaries of SSDI peaked in the late 1970s at just under 3 million, or about 15 percent more than after the most severe cutbacks in the early 1980s. There has been about a 10 percent increase since then. The number of all beneficiaries (disabled workers and dependents) reached 4.9 million before the cutbacks, fell to 3.7 million, and has risen very slowly thereafter (U.S. Department of Health and Human Services 1990a, 51). Chapter 3, and particularly Tables 3.2 through 3.6, include more comprehensive statistics concerning the growth in disability benefit programs.

someone who is disabled. The problems of blacks and other minority groups may seem distant from the lives of most Americans, and few experience long term unemployment or even short periods of poverty. But all feel a connection to the disabled. Even those who believe that most people on welfare are undeserving are not willing to indict the disabled as a class because it is a class to which they might belong. This emotional attachment to the disabled gives an extraordinary tone to the most ordinary discussions about this issue, making even small changes in disability benefit programs difficult to complete.[6]

Third, a strong disability rights movement emerged in the 1970s. The movement sought both to remove discriminatory barriers to employment among those who could work and to fight for better disability benefits among those who could not. The movement used people's emotional attachment to disability to its benefit, securing, in Section 504 of the Rehabilitation Act of 1973 and the Americans with Disabilities Act of 1990, a civil rights basis for its goals of nondiscrimination in accommodations, transportation, and employment and entitlement to benefits.[7]

Fourth, work disability has been implicated in every trend that troubles every person of every ideological stripe, including the aging of the population, declining mortality and rising morbidity, the transformation of the economy from manufacturing to services, the change in the composition of the labor force, declining real wages and rising real benefit rates, the growth in health and disability benefits in particular and in federal expenditures in general, and declining federal revenues.[8]

Fifth, though work disability is implicated in every worrisome trend, no one has made a compelling case that it is a cause or consequence of any of them. We still do not know why

[6]The importance of the emotional attachment that all of us have to disability rights issues was noted by Stone (1984, 192): "[The disabled] are a foreboding of what we all might become. . . . The disability rights movement forces us to contemplate ourselves as less than whole."

[7]See Scotch (1984, especially 139–168) for a discussion of the passage and subsequent implementation of Section 504, which applied to anyone receiving federal funds. More recently, the Americans with Disabilities Act barred discrimination in employment, transportation, and accommodations for all citizens. For a discussion of issues relating to its implementation, see Yelin (1991).

[8]See Yelin (1989) for a review of these trends.

individuals stop working in the face of illness, and we are still seeking a consistent explanation for the growth in this phenomenon. Thus, policymakers are drawn to the work disability issue because they see it as central to aging, health, and economic trends and because they recognize that disability programs, unlike other entitlements, are flexible and may be reduced. Once drawn to this issue, however, they are frustrated by the emotional fervor with which disability benefits are defended and by the refractory nature of the problem.

Ironically, concern about work disability has little to do with the plight of those who actually leave work in the presence of illness. Instead, work disability interests policymakers and academics because it is a window onto aging and social welfare issues. When those issues recede in importance, either because some other set of issues temporarily displaces them from public discussion or because program reforms in disability compensation postpone a crisis in entitlement, persons who have been displaced from the labor force by illness are displaced from view, even though their access to work may continue to worsen. The "real" problem of declining employment among persons with disabilities garners less attention than does the more abstract concern about the impact of population aging or the fiscal health of government.

Policymakers are not alone in expressing their interest in the problem of work disability, even if only temporarily: almost every academic discipline has also joined the debate, each with its own jargon. But the jargon merely obscures the essential similarities among the disciplines within two polar camps: the one holding that immutable need drives the increase in work disability rates; the other, that a quite mutable choice not to work accounts for this rise. For those in the former camp, medical need is rising in tandem with the aging of the population, which places more of us at risk for disability, and with the paradoxical shift from mortal conditions to morbid ones, which leaves more people of each age prey to disability.[9] Moreover, because persons with disabilities

[9]There are several cogent reviews of the impact of demographic and medical factors on the growth in disability rates. Colvez and Blanchet (1981) noted a dramatic increase in the proportion of adults claiming activity limitation. Verbrugge (1984) found that the long-term reduction in mortality rates was accompanied by rising rates of activity limitation due, paradoxically, to non-

are prone to be the last hired and first fired, high unemployment is accentuating the health trends in raising the work disability rate. For those in the choice camp, the rising value of disability benefits, especially relative to wage rates, is giving workers with minor health problems the opportunity to choose leisure over employment. The rules and regulations defining work capacity may be flexible, but that flexibility has existed since the first disability compensation programs were begun, even if we have not always recognized the flexibility. Only the incentive to bend the rules has changed. We are enticing persons with health problems to stop working by making leisure too profitable.[10]

The debate between those attributing the burgeoning work disability rates to medical need and those attributing them to personal choice sounds much like the discourse on human nature that might take place in an introductory undergraduate political science course. Is a medical condition an accident of nature that

---

mortal conditions. She later argued (Verbrugge 1989) that the rise in disability rates resulted in part from frail individuals' being kept alive by advances in medical care and in part from rising real rates of nonfatal conditions. Further, Chirikos (1986) ruled out changes in definitions of disability and propensity to claim activity limitation as sources of the growth in work disability (defined by him to mean capacity for work), suggesting that declining health accounts for the rise in the proportion of working-age adults who define themselves as unable to work. Finally, Rice and LaPlante (1988) found that rates of co-occurring conditions were increasing over time, and that this played a crucial role in fostering the rising disability rates.

[10]The choice model, sometimes called replacement rate theory, holds that persons with impairments will evaluate whether to work by taking into account the subjective value they attach to labor and leisure. Then they will calibrate the expected wage from work versus the expected amount of income received when out of work to proxy the internal value system, and this calculated value will affect the decision to drop out of the labor force. In 1986, I reviewed the literature on choice, finding that the reported effect of disability compensation varied tremendously in the studies, with the earlier studies finding a larger impact, and the later ones a much smaller (or no) effect. Interestingly, the later studies controlled for the medical characteristics of the individuals in a much more systematic fashion, suggesting that the effect found in the earlier studies was due to poor measurement of health risk, rather than the real impact of benefit programs (Yelin, 1986). See also Feldstein 1974; Parsons 1980; Haveman and Wolfe 1984; and Stern 1989. Tuma and Sandefur (1988) is the only recent study that shows much effect of disability compensation on labor force participation, but since that paper had poor measures of health status, it is the exception that proves the rule.

deprives the individual of fulfillment in work and in life, or does illness legitimate a withdrawal from responsibility and disability insurance make this lamentable strategy pay? Like other stylizations of human nature, the need and choice models of work disability may be useful in some circumstances. The construction worker left quadriplegic from an industrial accident cannot work and ought to receive compensation. The harried clerk in the civil service claiming mental strain, on the other hand, is probably malingering.[11] But neither case is readily applicable to that of the hard-of-hearing teacher.

Quadriplegia and stress-related illness have come to symbolize the polar positions on work disability in academic discourse and congressional debate.[12] Their utility in the political arena is well established. Anyone seeking to reduce expenditures for disability benefits will note the thousands of people compensated for stress; no attempt to defend work disability compensation can take place without hearing the testimony of the person with a crippling injury abruptly removed from the beneficiary rolls.

However, most of the persons applying for disability benefits have medical conditions with a more subtle impact on functioning than that of either quadriplegia or stress. And most of them hold jobs with a more complex set of requirements than those of the construction worker or clerk. Thus, the majority of claims for disability benefits are inherently problematic, involving judgments about the interaction of illnesses with slow onset and insidious progression and jobs with changing physical and mental requirements. The computer operator with tendonitis and the schoolteacher with hearing loss are much more common examples of contemporary claimants, their cases are more difficult to adjudicate, and they are unlikely symbols in anyone's political

[11]Medical need is inherently an absolutist model: there is a line and all those on one side of it get compensation. In that sense, the need model may be more applicable to the person with quadriplegia. Choice is inherently a relativist model: individuals equilibrate their love for work and leisure at the margin. In that sense, the choice model may be more applicable to those with marginal impairments.

[12]In the congressional hearings held in response to the removal of SSDI beneficiaries prior to appeal (U.S. Congress 1984a, 1984b), Senate and House staff brought persons with quadriplegia to Washington to demonstrate that truly "needy" individuals had been thrown off the SSDI rolls, and this proved helpful in getting the regulations mandating removal prior to appeal changed.

agenda. Neither condition would seem to preclude employment, although sustaining work with impairments and jobs like these would not be easy. Likewise, it is equally plausible that the prospect of receiving disability benefits would make the decision to leave work easier or that the $600 to $900 a month one might get by doing so would not be enough of an enticement.

Disability policy was founded on the notion that persons with medical need should be compensated for their poor luck, and it was reformed on the notion that individuals were choosing disability over work. Grounded in alternative visions of human nature, and developed in different eras with fundamentally different predispositions to state expenditure,[13] the polar models of need and choice nevertheless both fail to explain the rising pandemic of work disability encompassing such people as the computer operator with tendonitis and the schoolteacher with hearing loss.

A Workplace Model

In this book, I argue that the flexibility inherent in disability compensation programs is a necessary but not sufficient condition to explain the growth in work disability over the last two decades. Work disability compensation programs could not grow until persons with chronic conditions and their physicians increased their predisposition to claim benefits and the Social Security examiners representing the state increased their predisposition to grant them. That the chronically ill, their physicians, and Social Security examiners changed their predispositions is not in doubt: declining rates of labor force participation among the chronically ill and rising rates of disability entitlement, particularly in the 1970s, attest to this. What is in doubt is why and how these predispositions changed. This book locates the growth of work disability in changes within work and employment.

The physical basis of work has been eroding over the last several decades. This erosion has been in part a by-product of the shift from manufacturing to services. Although the fast food restaurant—perhaps the paradigm of contemporary service

[13] The political climate undermining social welfare expenditures during the last decade or so is explored in Marmor, Mashaw, and Harvey (1990, especially chap. 2, "The American Opportunity-Insurance State").

work—can be very physically demanding, on balance, work within services requires less physical exertion than in manufacturing. Moreover, manufacturing itself has become less demanding. In the initial phases of automation, the worker's body no longer provided power but controlled and focused the power of external sources. In the auto plant, for instance, the worker still riveted, but used a power tool to do it. In the more recent phase, the power is both externally provided and controlled, and the worker monitors production at some remove from the power source.[14] A robot may do the actually riveting, while the auto worker observes the process by watching a digital readout away from the point of assembly.

The growth in work disability rates stems not from changes in the physical demands of work, but rather from changes in the demand for specific kinds of labor. The transformation from manufacturing to services and the transformations within manufacturing presented employers and society with a problem: how to displace thousands (perhaps millions) of workers whose jobs were being eliminated because of automation or because their firms were no longer competitive. Most workers so displaced were older males, predominantly blue-collar employees of manufacturing firms without the skills (and perhaps without the desire) to find work in the service economy. The disability compensation system accommodated many of these workers in much the same way that early retirement programs accommodated white-collar workers displaced from middle management jobs in the same firms: by providing a soft landing through the relatively high levels of income disability programs confer (and which, by and large, employers do not pay for themselves) and by legitimating unemployment under the mantel of illness and disability. I imply no blame in using the term *legitimation*. Legitimation worked for the employer in so far as it eased workers out of the firm while externalizing the cost of doing so, and it worked for the employee who faced the prospect of long-term unemployment and drastic reduction in income.

Health and demographic dynamics abetted the legitimation process. The aging of the work force put more people at risk for

[14]See Zuboff (1988) and Hirschhorn (1984) for a discussion of the cybernetic factory.

chronic illness. In addition, the number reporting limitation in work capacity rose among people of every age, suggesting that the disability rate was increasing both because more were older and because more of all ages were sick. But the aging of the population and worsening health impede employment only if employers are unwilling to accommodate the special needs of their workers: working is possible despite all but the most severe chronic conditions. Employers are unwilling to make these accommodations when there is a surplus of labor. Thus, rising work disability rates reflect changes in the willingness of employers to accommodate the needs of workers with impairments rather than changes in the prevalence of illness or impairment. Indeed, limitation in work capacity due to chronic disease was once much less of an impediment to employment than in recent years. As we shall see in Chapter 2, as recently as two decades ago, men aged 55–64 with work limitations (the group at highest risk for work disability) were about 20 percent more likely to keep working as today.

The willingness of employers to accommodate the special needs of their workers ebbs and flows with the overall demand for labor in the economy, but the impact will be greatest in industries undergoing rapid expansion and contraction. Fast food franchises, facing a severe shortage of labor, are glad to hire and then accommodate workers with severe impairments. Many manufacturing firms, in contrast, are asking workers without impairments to accept more stringent working conditions and substantial reductions in income.

The thesis of this book is that the rise in work disability rates is concentrated among workers in industries undergoing contraction and has occurred because firms in these industries fail to make the accommodations necessary for persons with impairments to continue working and because the firms and their employees can call upon the disability compensation system to buffer unemployment. The thesis neither implies that the displaced workers do not or should not qualify for the disability benefits they may ultimately receive, nor that the disability benefits act as an enticement, drawing workers with impairments away from employment. The number of workers who would qualify for disability benefits has always exceeded the number who apply for them.[15] Moreover, the

---

[15]See Lando, Cutler, and Gamber 1982; and Yelin 1989.

evidence that disability compensation programs entice workers to leave their jobs is, at best, weak.[16]

If changes in the structure of employment account for much of the historical rise in work disability rates, the structure of work is also responsible for determining who will stop working in the presence in illness at any given point in time: very few medical conditions preclude all employment. However, it is not the physical demands of jobs that are critical: very few jobs in the contemporary economy require a level of physical exertion that chronic disease precludes. Instead, the fit between the time characteristics of illness and the time characteristics of the job are far more important in determining whether work loss will result from an impairment.[17] Most chronic conditions have alternating periods of exacerbation and remission, lasting days, weeks, or even months. During the exacerbations, the individual with a chronic condition may need to withdraw from work in order to rest and secure medical care. During the remissions, the individual may have the energy to make up for lost time, or at least to resume a more normal work load. Individuals with jobs allowing them the flexibility to schedule illness exacerbations and attendant medical care around work are much likelier to continue working despite their conditions. Individuals with inflexible jobs, in contrast, have higher work disability rates.

The fit between the time requirements of chronic illness and work has been poorest in the manufacturing sector; this misfit, rather than the brute force requirements of manufacturing-based employment, accounts for the higher work disability rates in that set of industries. The paradox is that the inflexible work rules are no longer a necessary part of manufacturing. Indeed, successful manufacturing seems to require discretion, autonomy, and flexibility in working conditions to accomplish its goals. Thus, manufacturing is responsible for a disproportionate share of the growth in work disability rates across time and for a disproportionate share of work disability at the current time, but for unexpected reasons. Work disability rates have been growing not be-

16The most comprehensive studies of this phenomenon indicate that disability compensation resulted in a decline of 1 percentage point in older male labor force participation rates (see Haveman and Wolfe 1984) or that there is no effect whatsoever (Yelin 1986).

17This argument is developed in Yelin, Nevitt, and Epstein (1980).

cause manufacturing requires more physical exertion but because manufacturing has inflexible work rules. In turn, the inflexible work rules are a double cause of disability: in the short term because they preclude the accommodation to illness necessary for the person with chronic disease to maintain employment, and in the long-term because inflexible work rules are emblematic of outmoded manufacturing that displaces workers in the wake of its failure to compete in the marketplace.

Some people acquire illnesses that render them incapable of work. Some with illnesses cynically manipulate the disability compensation system. We tend to remember both sets of individuals because they symbolize the notions of pure need and pure greed. But both are statistically rare. Most of those who leave jobs do so for more prosaic reasons: because their illnesses make negotiating work rules difficult, because they are being displaced from work, or through a combination of these factors.

My goal in this book is to demonstrate that the structure of work and employment is the proper locus for work disability policy and to redirect attention away from the unresolvable and pointless debate as to whether medical need or personal choice to withdraw from work is responsible for work disability. In so doing, I will show that work disability, like many other social problems, arises from our failure to master the technologies of manufacture and thereby sustain the demand for the kind of high-wage labor historically associated with the manufacturing sector. Thus, work disability may be the perfect reflection of our troubled economy. If so, we might better focus on the sources of slow growth and on a more general set of employment and social welfare policies to accommodate these economic changes than on work disability policy per se. My guess is that we choose the more narrow emphasis on individuals—either their medical characteristics or their proclivity to choose leisure over labor—because it is far easier to eliminate people from the disability rolls or reduce the benefits of those who remain beneficiaries than to generate higher incomes across the entire labor force. Whether or not this is so, I argue here that several million people with illness of unquestioned severity have suffered from the unwarranted attacks on their eligibility for disability compensation. Establishing that the rise in work disability resides, even partially, in the transformation of the economy might help to get this monkey off their backs.

Organization of the Book

At its height in the late 1970s, the Social Security Disability Insurance (SSDI) program paid benefits to more than 2 percent of the U.S. population. The number of beneficiaries has since fallen, both absolutely and relatively. However, the number of persons claiming an inability to work due to illness and the number who have actually left work after onset of illness have continued to climb, suggesting that the reforms in SSDI were, at best, a temporary solution and that pressure for program expansion remains. Chapters 2 and 3 explore the trends fueling the ongoing increase in work disability. Chapter 2 describes the aging of the population and change in the health of people of each age (read "need"), and Chapter 3 charts the changes in the number of persons receiving disability compensation, the size of their benefits, and the relationship of their benefits to salaries and wages (read "choice"). Neither set of data supports a simple explanation. The health of workers in the immediate preretirement years is indeed worsening as the entire population ages, but these trends account for only a small fraction of the growth in the number of persons leaving work because of illness. Indeed, the group with the worst decline in health—older women—had the smallest change in work disability rates, while the group with the smallest change in health—older men—experienced dramatically higher work disability rates. Moreover, the level of disability benefits has had little impact on the labor force participation rate. Thus, neither the need nor the choice model explains the explosive growth in work disability programs.

Chapter 4 examines the effects of labor market changes. Over the last three decades, the composition of the labor force has undergone dramatic shifts. In 1960, over 93 percent of men were in the labor force, but by 1988 this proportion had declined to 88 percent. Over the same time period, women's labor force participation rate increased by more than 50 percent (reaching 68 percent of all women). These overall shifts tell only part of the story: most of the decline in male labor force participation has occurred among older men, and a disproportionate amount of this occurred among older nonwhite men. Most of the increase in women's labor force participation, in contrast, was concentrated among younger women, particularly white women. Chapter 4 charts the quantitative changes in the labor market over the last two decades, showing how the shift to service sector employment was accompanied by a loss of employment security, thereby setting the stage for the displacement of persons with disabilities from the labor market.

Chapter 5 shifts the focus from macro trends in employment over the last several decades to changes within work itself, or to be more precise, to changes that should have occurred for the betterment of the U.S. economy, but did not. To do this, it contrasts the structure of work in U.S. factories during much of this century with the structure used in factories organized around the principles of continuous feedback and improvement. In the former, work is set by design. In the latter, workers are encouraged to learn and to change the process of manufacture as they learn. I show that work in such environments allows the kind of flexibility persons with disabilities need to stay on the job despite illness and that, paradoxically, factories organized on these principles are also more successful. Thus, whether because the working conditions in the old factory are incompatible with the rhythms of chronic disease, or because the firms that rely on them are not as successful, the result is the same: persons with disabilities are at risk for displacement from their jobs.

Chapter 6 retraces the employment dynamics summarized in Chapters 4 and 5, this time showing how that the person with disability is, regrettably, on the leading edge of both the macro and micro changes in work. First, I demonstrate that, like race and gender, disability status accentuates changes going on in employment. Thus, while older men in general are seeing their labor force participation rates decline, nonwhite older men and those with disabilities experience a disproportionate loss of employment, which in the latter case gets called work disability. And while younger women enter the labor force in record numbers, nonwhite younger women and those with disabilities do not share equally in these gains. These changes at the macro level reach the shop floor, with older men with work disabilities suffering displacement from the contracting sectors of the economy, and they also reach the service industries, with younger women with disabilities taking what work is left over.

Chapter 7 analyzes employment policy in general and disability policy in particular in light of the two principal findings of the book: that health accentuates the overall trends in employment and that disability policy has been used, albeit implicitly, to accommodate the shift from manufacturing to service employment. I argue that traditional disability compensation programs, including SSDI, fail because they attempt to put a medical slant on problems of displacement from the labor force and should, instead, meld disability compensation with Social Security retirement for workers with impairments over age 50, in effect using the SSDI trust to fund a program of early retirement payments at reduced levels for those choosing this route. Such a change would acknowledge that disability compensation can never be separated from more general employment and income dynamics, and would be designed to reduce the state's role as a disability compensation police force.

However, reforming SSDI is only a minor part of a strategy—and a relatively uncreative one at that—to focus work disability policy on the workplace. Chapter 7 also describes some of the policies that business, labor, and government can jointly initiate to improve the chances that persons with chronic conditions will be able to stay at work. These initiatives are based on the notion that the public and private sectors can do much to create safe harbors for persons with disabilities in the high-wage, growth industries of the 1990s, thus extricating policymaking from both the passive stance that we are about to be overtaken by demographic forces out of control and the more active one that work disability is generated by public entitlement programs.

2

Aging, Health, and Work Capacity

The demographer Richard Easterlin [1980] (1987) argued that the relative size of a generation has become a principal and arguably the most important determinant of an individual's behavior and well-being. The baby bust generation of the Depression suffered initially, but then experienced phenomenal economic growth spread across their relatively few members. This success allowed them to have many children and to do so early. In contrast, their children, the baby boomers, were forced to divvy up resources among a greater number. The baby boomers then delayed having children because establishing their careers took a long time. In this manner, a small generation begat a large generation and so on, propagating alternate waves of relative affluence and impoverishment. Accordingly, the reproductive habits of one's parents—indeed, of one's grandparents—dictate the well-being of one's generation.

Easterlin's theory permeates almost all discussions of economics and social welfare these days, if only implicitly and if only because the notion that the number of slices determines a generation's fate seems so germane when the size of the pie remains fixed. Much of this discussion focuses on the impact of financing Social Security and medical care for the elderly, but increasingly analysts are turning to the impact of demographic changes on labor force behavior as well, seeing in the aging of the population the inevitable march of frailty and subsequently of work disability.

This chapter asks if a graying work force necessarily means

growing work disability rates and answers that it does not. Gray workers once toiled at very physically demanding jobs, and neither their growing numbers nor their declining health explain why they no longer hold the less strenuous jobs of the service economy. High rates of labor force participation among older workers, even among those with health problems, are not ancient history. As recently as two decades ago, the majority with severe impairments worked until the traditional age of retirement.

Population aging has begun to garner a lot of attention in the popular and academic press—belatedly, since the population has been aging for close to a century. Most of this analysis is irrelevant to discussions of the labor market, dealing instead with the health of people in the last years of life and emphasizing the burden of supporting an increasing number of very frail old through economic transfers and unloving care.[1] The emphasis on the very old is misplaced because the principal effect of population aging has been to shift the median age from late childhood to early adulthood, thereby swelling the ranks of the middle-aged, not the elderly. Moreover, the emphasis on the elderly obscures a substantial decline in the health of the middle-aged in recent years, a decline with much more profound implications for the labor market today and for the well-being of the elderly tomorrow. The worsening health status of persons in late middle age was easy to miss, representing slowly increasing rates of slowly progressing nonfatal conditions, such as arthritis, osteoporosis, and slight neurological impairment, rather than dramatic increases in dramatic, fatal conditions, such as heart disease, cancer, and stroke. Once noticed, however, these trends fueled fears that a pandemic of work disability was around the corner, and that the invisible hand of demography and illness would clear the labor market of older workers.

Past Demographic Trends

As the twentieth century began, the United States was predominantly a society of the young. It was young because of the con-

---

[1]The extent to which the nonelderly can or should pay for health services and long-term care for the elderly has been the subject of debate among economists and bioethicists. See, for example, Aaron and Schwartz 1984; Rivlin and Wiener 1988; Callahan 1990; and Daniels 1988.

Table 2.1. U.S. Birth Rates, 1900–1987

Year	No. live births (millions)	Birth rate (per 1,000 persons)
1900	2.280	30.0
1920	2.950	27.7
1940	2.559	19.4
1960	4.258	23.7[a]
1980	3.612	15.9[b]
1987	3.829	15.7

Sources: Author's calculations from U.S. Bureau of the Census 1976, 15, 49; id. 1989a, 59.

[a]Postwar birth rates peaked in 1957, at 25.3/1,000 persons.

[b]The twentieth-century birth rate was at its minimum in 1975 and 1976, at 14.6/1,000 persons.

fluence of sustained high birth rates and declining infant mortality, and because of the youth of the large number of immigrants.[2] In the first decade of this century, for example, the birth rate was approximately twice what it is now (Table 2.1),[3] and the infant mortality rate, though many times what it is now, had already begun its descent (Table 2.2).[4] In that same decade, almost nine million people moved to the United States, swelling the population by over 10 percent net of natality and mortality. But as the birth rate declined in concert with declining infant mortality, and as the mass immigration was choked off, the population began to age. Declining mortality among the elderly, particularly in the last two decades, abetted this trend, but demographers attach more importance to the earlier decreases in the birth rate than to these more recent developments, citing the greater relative

[2]See, for example, Stolnitz (1964) and Coale (1964) for an explanation of how declining birth and death rates result in an older population.

[3]Table 2.1 displays birth rates in the United States throughout this century.

[4]Table 2.2 portrays the decline in death rates for persons of different ages. The death rate of children under age 1 has declined by more than 90 percent since 1900, whereas the death rate among adults aged 55–64, 65–74, and 75–84 has declined by about half. Most of the decline in death rates among children occurred in the first decades of this century; the decline among adults has accelerated in recent decades, however.

Table 2.2. U.S Death Rates by Age, 1900–1987
(deaths per 1,000 persons)

			Age Group		
Year	Under 1	55–64	65–74	75–84	85 and over[1]
1900	162.4	27.2	56.4	123.4	260
1920	92.3	23.6	52.5	118.9	248
1940	54.9	22.2	48.4	112.0	235
1960	27.0	17.4	38.2	87.5	198
1980	12.9	13.5	30.0	66.9	159.8
1987	10.2	13.4	27.5	62.8	153.2

Sources: Author's calculations from U.S Bureau of the Census 1976, 60; U.S. Department of Health and Human Services 1985a, 38; id. 1989a, table 20.

[a]Published death rates for 1900–1960 for persons over age 85 are not calculated with the same precision as those for the younger age groups.

increase in life expectancy at birth than at age 65 as proof (Table 2.3).[5]

The consistent aging of the U.S. population during the twentieth century is clearly visible in Figure 2.1. In 1900, more than 80 percent of the population were under 44 years old, and more than 40 percent were under 20. Only one in twenty-five people was over 65, about three million in all. Since then, the proportion of the young has declined steadily—with the exception of the period following the postwar baby boom—and the proportion of the elderly has trebled. There are now about thirty million elders, a fact not lost on those who view segments of the population in terms of market potential. The median age has risen in tandem with these trends, from about 23 in 1900 to 32 as of 1987, making us a nation neither of children nor of elders.

Indeed, population aging does not dramatically alter the proportion of people of working ages. In 1900, 52 percent of the population were between 20 and 65; since then, those of working ages have never constituted fewer than 54 percent of the people. Moreover, the number of workers between 20 and 44 has always dwarfed the number between 45 and 64 and will do so for the foreseeable future. Discussions of the aging of the work force

[5]The data concerning the relative increases in life expectancy at birth and age 65 are presented in greater detail in Verbrugge (1989).

Table 2.3. Life Expectancy of the U.S. Population at Birth and
at Age 65, 1900–1987 (years)

Year	At birth	At age 65
1900	47.3	11.9
1920	54.1	12.2
1940	62.9	12.8
1960	69.7	14.3
1980	73.7	16.4
1987 (proj.)	75.0	16.9

Sources: Author's calculations from U.S. Bureau of the Census 1976, 55; id. 1984a, 59; U.S. Department of Health and Human Services 1985a, 40.

notwithstanding, in 1987 about two-thirds of working-age individuals were in the first half of their careers.

Population aging also does not necessarily increase the proportion of people who are not of working age. The so-called dependency ratio—the number of persons under 20 or over 65 divided by the number between these ages—has fluctuated throughout the century, but it reached an historical low in 1987. The composition of the nonworking-age population shifts with aging, however. In

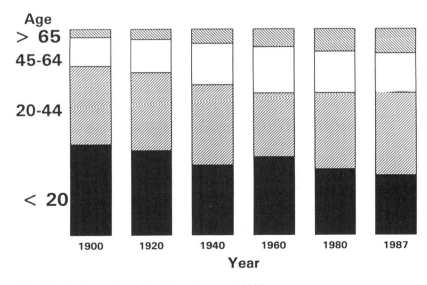

Fig. 2.1 Aging of the U.S. Population, 1900–1987
Source: Author's calculations from U.S. Bureau of the Census 1976, 16, 19; id. 1989a, 17.

1900, there were 11 children for every elder, a ratio that has fallen steadily since, reaching 2.4 as of 1987. Gradually, we find ourselves paying more for Social Security and Medicare and less for schooling, and because public expenditures on behalf of an elderly person are greater than those for a child, the costs of the nonworking-age population have risen in both absolute and relative terms.[6]

Future Demographic Trends

The graying of the nonworking population is likely to continue for the next half-century, although in every projected scenario the proportion of the population of working age will greatly exceed the total dependent population. Indeed, dependency ratios during the twenty-first century will be, on average, much lower than those of the twentieth.

Table 2.4 projects population dynamics between 2000 and 2040, using alternative assumptions of slow or fast population growth. In all likelihood, these projections bracket the true population for those years. Under either assumption, the proportion over age 85 will double (albeit to only 5 percent or less of the population) and the proportion aged 65–85 will increase to between 16 and 20 percent. Since most of those who will be of working age during this time span are already alive, we know, too, that the proportion of the total population of working age will never exceed 63 percent (occurring in the year 2000) or fall below 54 percent (in 2040, if and only if population growth continues at a fast pace). However, the proportion of the population in the first half of their careers will decline, whatever the overall rate of population growth, from about 40 percent in the year 2000 to no more than 33 percent in 2040. And even assuming continual fast population growth, the proportion of the population in childhood will never approach twentieth-century levels, so the number of new entrants into the labor force also will fall.

The proportion of older workers staying in the labor force has been declining for several decades, but workers beginning their careers have been available to replace them. Since this will no longer be the case, labor shortages are likely to occur unless older

[6]See, for example, Clark and Spengler 1978; Sheppard and Rix 1979; Foner and Schwab 1983; and Preston 1984.

Table 2.4. Projected Age Structure of the U.S. Population, 2000–2040 (percent of population)

Year	Nature of growth	Age Group: Under 18	18–44	45–64	65–85	Over 85
2000	Slow	24	40	23	11	2
	Fast	26	39	23	11	2
2020	Slow	19	35	28	16	2
	Fast	24	34	24	15	3
2040	Slow	17	32	27	20	4
	Fast	24	33	21	16	5

Source: Author's calculations from U.S. Bureau of the Census 1989c, 8.

workers can be convinced to continue working, have the requisite skills for the jobs that will be available, and will be healthy enough to stay in the labor market. The fear that older persons will be too frail to work cannot be separated from the fear that the small post–baby boom cohorts will not be sufficiently large to replenish the labor force.

Past and Future Health Trends

Death rates among the elderly have declined by a quarter or more over the last several decades (see Table 2.2). This fact of history has prompted much discussion about the health of the increasing numbers of those who have survived to old age and much speculation about the health of those who will survive in years to come. There seems to be little question that overall disability rates have risen, more so for middle-aged persons than for the elderly, but there is little consensus about what this means for the future. One analyst claims that the decline in disability rates should soon parallel decreases in death rates, albeit at a lag of a decade or two, eventually compressing the period of morbidity prior to death.[7]

[7]James Fries has been the principal proponent of this thesis, first arguing a decade ago that the average length of human life is fixed, that the proportion living close to the end of this fixed life span is increasing, and that the delay in the onset of the chronic conditions of aging will compress the duration of morbidity (Fries 1980). Subsequently, he has recanted somewhat, holding that there is good evidence that prevention can compress morbidity but that the

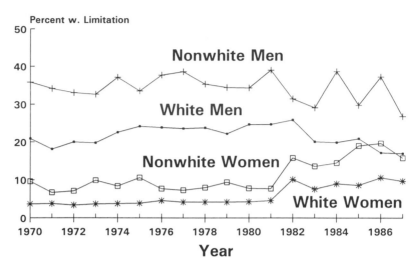

Fig. 2.2   Disability Rates of Persons Aged 65–69 by Race and Sex, U.S., 1970–1987
Source: Author's analysis of National Health Interview Survey data.

Others argue that the duration of morbidity will be extended as delayed mortality exposes more of us to progressively worsening nonfatal conditions.[8] Still others hold that eventually morbidity and mortality may reach a new equilibrium similar to that which existed prior to the recent reduction in mortality rates, but that this scenario has not yet come to pass. In this view, the period of disability prior to death will eventually approximate that of earlier eras, but will occur with later onset of disability and later death.[9]

Figures 2.2 through 2.4 chart the trends in severe disability over the last two decades in the United States for the young elderly (those aged 65–69) and persons of late middle age (45–54 and 55–65), all of whom might, conceivably, work. The data derive from the National Health Interview Survey, an annual, cross-sectional

compression of morbidity is an attainable goal if and only if we choose to invest in prevention strategies (Fries 1988, 1989).

[8]The pessimistic position that the confluence of declining mortality and acute illness results in increasing disability due to degenerative chronic conditions was first spelled out by Ernest Gruenberg (1977) and soon thereafter buttressed with some preliminary data by Morton Kramer (1980).

[9]See, for example, Manton 1982; Olshansky and Ault 1986; Olshansky 1990.

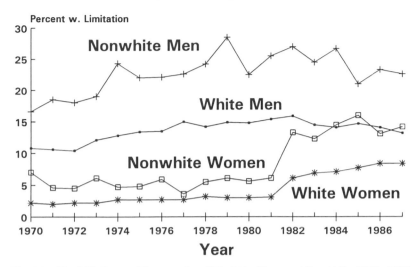

Fig. 2.3   Disability Rates of Persons Aged 55–64 by Race and Sex, U.S., 1970–1987
Source: Author's analysis of National Health Interview Survey data.

look at the U.S. population living outside of institutions.[10] Among persons aged 65–69 (Figure 2.2), disability rates have not changed dramatically with the passage of time. Indeed, disability rates among white men appear to have fallen slightly in recent years; rates among nonwhite men, though more volatile, have held steady; and rates among white and nonwhite women have risen, albeit very slightly. Thus, the typical elderly person—at least if between 65 and 69—is in roughly the same shape as two decades ago, perhaps a little better off if a man and a little worse if a woman.

The picture is very different for persons aged 55–64. The proportion claiming severe disability has risen substantially since 1970 for both white and nonwhite men; risen steadily among white women, and perhaps risen slightly among nonwhite women (Figure 2.3). Even after slight declines in recent years, about 25 and 35 percent more white and nonwhite men, respectively, in

[10]The definition of disability used in the National Health Interview changed in 1982, artificially inflating disability rates for women thereafter. This did not affect the trends among women before or after 1982, however. Despite the large sample size of this survey, the estimates of disability rates among nonwhites are unstable. The conservative strategy would be to place more emphasis on long-term trends than on estimates for any one year.

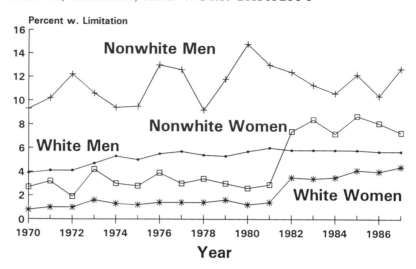

Fig. 2.4   Disability Rates of Persons Aged 45–54 by Race and Sex, U.S., 1970–1987
Source: Author's analysis of National Health Interview Survey data.

this age group report severe activity limitations than in the early 1970s. All told, about one-quarter of nonwhite men of these ages claim severe limitation of activity. White women aged 55 to 64 report much lower rates of severe activity limitation than those of men, but their disability rates have been increasing, suggesting that as they become more active participants in the labor market, their disability profile may come to resemble others with a substantial work history. Prior to the 1982 change in the definition of disability for women in the National Health Interview, rates of severe activity limitation among white women aged 55 to 64 increased by 50 percent. If one were to project the 1970–1982 increases to 1987, white women of these ages would have experienced a 75 percent increase in severe activity limitation rates. Since 1982, their rates of severe activity limitation have increased by one-quarter. Even discounting some of this increase as an artifact of the definitions of disability in the survey, one can safely argue that white women aged 55 to 64 have experienced dramatic growth in severe disability. Rates of severe activity limitation among nonwhite women aged 55 to 64 held steady prior to 1982 and seem to have risen on average in the interim. They continue to be substantially higher than the rates among white women.

Disability rates also increased among persons aged 45–54 (Figure 2.4), the time in life when labor force participation rates peak. Nonwhite men of these ages experience the highest rates of activity limitation (over 10 percent), but, on average, have sustained no major change in their rates of severe activity limitation since 1970. The average, however, masks tremendous volatility. It is of interest that the prevalence of severe activity limitation among nonwhite men aged 45 to 54 decreased throughout much of the 1980s, which suggests that reporting of activity limitation was not being used to legitimate unemployment rates during this period. The rate of severe activity limitation among nonwhite women aged 45 to 54 also did not change much between 1970 and 1982, but may have risen on average since. White men and white women of these ages, on the other hand, have both experienced steady increases in rates of severe activity limitation: perhaps 20 percent among white men, about 30 percent among white women prior to 1982, and perhaps another 15 percent in the subsequent five years.

These trends in disability rates among working-age adults are troubling for several reasons. First, if disability rates rise among working-age adults while mortality rates decline among elders, both the prevalence and duration of disability will increase, validating the notion that we may substitute a pandemic of disability for high rates of mortality. Second, the baby boom generation will soon reach late working ages, their huge numbers putting intense pressure on the disability compensation system. Finally, the baby bust generation that follows may not be sufficient in size to compensate for the increased proportion of baby boomers who may have stopped working for health reasons, leaving a severe shortage in the labor market.

As is often the case in controversial fields of inquiry, several analysts caution that the apparent rise in disability rates may be artifactual (that is, dependent on the definition of disability[11] and/or on an increased propensity to claim inability to work),[12] temporary (that is, the short-term adjustment to a dramatic change

[11]See, for example, Wilson and Drury 1984.

[12]See, for example, Parsons 1980, 1991; Boskin and Hurd 1990; Tuma and Sandefur 1988.

in the prevalence of fatal conditions),[13] or limited (that is, the result of a process that has run its course),[14] While they are no doubt correct that the data concerning disability are imperfect, and that past trends may not continue into the future, the weight of the imperfect evidence already amassed suggests that the increase in disability rates over the last two decades is not artifactual.[15] Thus, the aging of the population puts more people at risk for disability, and a higher proportion of those at risk experience disability.

Health and the Labor Market

In a mechanical medical model of disability, aging and increases in the prevalence of chronic disease expose more workers to disability, but the shift within manufacturing to automated production and from manufacturing to services can put a brake on this trend by making work less physically demanding, thereby allowing persons with disabilities to stay employed. While the physical demands of work clearly have been reduced over the last

[13]This is the argument underlying the work of Manton (1982) and Olshansky and Ault 1986; and Olshansky 1990.

[14]Martynas Ycas (1988), for example, found that the increases in age-adjusted disability rates have slowed in the 1980s.

[15]Several lengthy reviews of the evidence concerning disability rates have been published in the last several years (Yelin 1989; Chirikos 1986; Verbrugge 1989; Crimmins and Pramaggione 1988; Rice and LaPlante 1988; and Chapman, LaPlante, and Wilensky 1986. Yelin (1989) notes that while severe disability rates have increased among working-age adults, overall disability rates have not. If propensity to report were to blame for increased rates of disability, rates of mild limitation would have risen more quickly, since these are the contestable cases. Moreover, prevalence rates of chronic conditions causing limitation have not risen uniformly. If the prevalence of all chronic conditions rose in tandem, one could argue that people are systematically more likely to report being ill. Since the prevalence of only some conditions rose, this makes reporting bias an unlikely source of the entire rise in disability rates (see Verbrugge 1984). Although most analysts rely on the Health Interview Survey and all using the Health Interview Survey concur in finding increased disability rates over all or part of the last two decades (Colvez and Blanchet 1981; Verbrugge 1984; Ycas 1988; Rice and LaPlante 1988; Chirikos 1986; Weinberger et al. 1986), analysts using other sources also reported increased rates of disability (Chirikos [1986] reviews these sources).

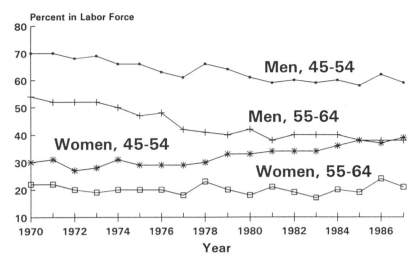

Fig. 2.5   Labor Force Participation of Persons with Disabilities by Sex and Age, U.S., 1970–1987
Source: Author's analysis of National Health Interview Survey data.

two decades,[16] the overall proportion of persons with disabilities in the labor force, net of severe declines among men and increases among some women, has continued to decline. Deindustrialization has not compensated for increased disability rates.

Figure 2.5 summarizes these dynamics. In 1970 about 70 percent of men aged 45–54 with activity limitation reported themselves as being in the labor force, a proportion that fell about 10 percent as the 1980s progressed. Men aged 55–64 with activity limitations sustained a much larger fall in their labor force participation, from 55 percent in 1970 to 40 percent in 1987, a decline of more than a quarter in relative terms.[17] In sharp contrast, labor force participation among women aged 55–64 with activity limitation held steady throughout the period under study,

[16]This statement would be true if, as has been the case, the distribution of occupations and industries shifted to less physically demanding ones without any reduction in the physical requirements of each occupation and industry (U.S. Bureau of the Census 1989a, 388–389).

[17]Figures 6.1 through 6.4 in Chapter 6 indicate that the declining labor force participation of nonwhite men with activity limitation was more severe than these overall figures would indicate.

and the proportion of women aged 45–54 with such limitation actually increased substantially, from 30 percent in 1970 to more than 40 percent in 1987.

In the medical model of work disability, increased rates of activity limitation result in decreased labor force participation. The data just reviewed contravene the model since older women sustained larger increases in rates of activity limitation and, depending on their age, either steady or increased rates of labor force participation, while men experienced smaller changes in health status and a substantial falloff in labor force participation.

Between 1970 and 1986, the U.S. labor force underwent a dramatic series of transformations. Buffeted by the most severe recession since World War II, unemployment rates hit a forty year high in 1982 and 1983, but then "the Great American Jobs Machine"[18] took over, lowering the unemployment rate by more than half in the ensuing four years by generating over six million additional jobs. The labor force was feminized, too, with the proportion of women working growing by a quarter, growth that increased women's share of the overall labor force from 38 percent in 1970 to 45 percent in 1986. Chapters 4 and 5 discuss these labor market dynamics in much greater detail, while Chapter 6 describes their implications for the person with disabilities. For now, I want to emphasize that the prevalence of work disability did not change in direct relation to changes in health status, at least as measured by activity limitation, and that the aging of the population does not necessarily crowd out older workers, at least as evidenced by the increasing proportion of the working-age population in the labor force. Nevertheless, the overall expansion of the labor force did little to stem the decline in employment among older men generally, but especially among older men with disabilities. Masked by the feminization of the work force that was occurring at the same time, and unfolding much more slowly than the recession and recovery, the withdrawal of the older male worker with disability from work became a silent epidemic.

[18]The phrase "the Great American Jobs Machine", coined to indicate that in contrast to other developed nations, ours has a low unemployment rate, was incorporated into a 1986 report (Bluestone and Harrison 1986) to lampoon the notion that it is possible to evaluate the quantity of employment separately from its quality.

Summary

The population of the United States has been aging almost since the inception of the nation over two centuries ago, but the main effect of this has been to raise the median age of the population to slightly more than 30, thus placing the typical citizen in the early stages of a four-decade career, and keeping a plurality of the labor force in the first half of their working lives. In the next half-century, however, there will be fewer workers between 18 and 44 relative to those between 45 and 64, igniting the fear of labor shortages if the trend for older workers to withdraw from the labor force continues. The increase in disability rates among persons 45 to 64 appears particularly worrisome when viewed in conjunction with these demographic shifts, because it raises the specter that older workers may begin to withdraw from the labor force at increasingly early ages, further tightening the demand for workers and raising the cost of labor in the process.

This notion that demography, abetted by disability, destines the nation to a labor shortage rests on the assumption that too many older workers do not want to work and that too many others cannot work. A recent survey of retirees, however, found that only half would choose to remain out of the labor force if sufficient opportunities for employment were available.[19] Of the remaining half, about one-third claimed a disability of some sort, and two-thirds simply had given up searching for work. The latter two-thirds represent a considerable contingent labor force, available to work in the right circumstances. I would argue that many of the disabled third do so as well. Large majorities of older workers with activity limitations worked as recently as the early 1970s, and the decline in their labor force participation occurred as the physical basis of employment eroded, a process that should have increased rates of participation. Demographic changes placed more persons at risk for disability, and rising disability rates placed more older persons at risk of work loss, but neither old age nor disability precludes employment, as the situation little more than a decade ago attests. I turn now to the alternative hypothesis, that rising entitlement accounts for the withdrawal of persons with activity limitation from the labor force.

---

[19]See Commonwealth Fund 1990.

3

The Social Context of the Work Disability Problem

Trends in the Social Security Disability Insurance Program (SSDI), the main entitlement program for persons with disabilities, can be understood only within the social and political context of the last decade or so. I argue that SSDI garnered as much attention as it did not because its size was a problem but because it provided a convenient target for conservatives arguing that government was simultaneously to blame for the decline of the American work ethic and for the economic stagnation of the 1970s. I show that SSDI cannot be held accountable for the withdrawal from work and thus was falsely maligned for its role in more general economic trends.

Filling the Post-Keynesian Vacuum

When times seem bad, or merely unfathomable, the consensus surrounding public policy begins to break down, creating a window of opportunity for competing notions of how society and the economy should be organized. When the Depression undermined the idea that markets for labor and capital are inherently self-regulating, the notion that government can steer the economy provided a clear alternative, smoothing the transition from laissez-faire capitalism to the welfare state. Indeed, some of the underpinnings for the welfare state already had been around for seventy-five years when the Depression hit, particularly the idea that social expenditures could soften the rough edges of industrial capitalism.[1] In retrospect, Keynes's suggestion that state expenditures can dampen economic cycles seems a small, albeit logical, extension of the idea that they can help the individual cope with those cycles.

No such blueprint was available when a quarter-century of steady economic growth ended in the early 1970s, ushering in close to a decade of low rates of growth combined with high rates of inflation. In the absence of a coherent way of understanding these disquieting economic developments, let alone dealing with them in a systematic fashion, statecraft had lost its legitimacy. The advocates for the reemergence of laissez-faire seized the chance to fill the vacuum, arguing that state expenditures simultaneously absorbed too much investment capital and sapped individuals' willingness to work.[2] George Gilder (1981, 111) writes:

> The moral hazards of current programs are clear. Unemployment compensation promotes unemployment. Aid for Families with Dependent Children makes more families dependent and fatherless. Disability insurance in all its multiple forms encourages the promotion of small ills into total and permanent ones. . . . Comprehensive Employment and Training Act subsidies for make-work may enhance a feeling of dependence on the state without giving the sometimes bracing experience of genuine work. All means-tested programs . . . promote the value of being "poor" and thus perpetuate poverty. To the degree that the moral hazards exceed the welfare effects, all these programs should be modified, usually by reducing the benefits.

Charles Murray (1984, 227–228) was willing to go one step farther and do away with entitlement programs completely:

[1]In response to the attack conservatives mounted on the welfare state in recent years, there has been a surge in good research demonstrating the effect of social welfare expenditures in reducing poverty (see Danziger and Plotnick [1982]; Blank and Blinder [1986]; Ellwood [1988] for the case for overall welfare expenditures; see Haveman and Wolfe [1989] for the case for disability expenditures) and even lending support to the now heretical position that social programs ameliorate the causes of poverty (see Schorr and Schorr [1988] and Lockhart [1989] for the general argument, and Burkhauser and Hirvonen [1989] for a discussion of disability programs, such as rehabilitation).

[2]This summary draws upon Fred Block's (1987) article "Rethinking the Political Economy of the Welfare State."

I begin with the proposition that it is within our resources to do enormous good for some people quickly. We have available to us a program that would convert a large proportion of the younger generation of hardcore unemployed into steady workers and [would help them] make a living wage. The same program would drastically reduce births to single teenage girls. It would measurably increase the upward socioeconomic mobility of poor families. These improvements would affect some millions of persons. The proposed program, our final and most ambitious thought experiment, consists of scrapping the entire Federal welfare and income-support structure for working-age persons, including AFDC, Medicaid, Food Stamps, Unemployment Insurance, Worker's Compensation, subsidized housing, disability insurance, and the rest. It would leave the working-aged person with no recourse whatsoever except the job market, family members, friends, and public or private locally funded services. It is the Alexandrian solution: cut the knot, for there is no way to untie it.

Although Gilder and Murray are equal opportunity critics of entitlement programs, opposing all of them, they reserve a disproportionate amount of their venom for publicly funded disability insurance. Disability compensation bears the brunt of this attack because of the absolute growth in the number of benefi ciaries and amount of expenditures on their behalf during the 1970s, because this growth was coincident with the economic stagnation of that period, because benefit payments were growing when wages were shrinking, because people tied these phenomena together, and because disability, unlike other entitlement criteria, is a contingent state, making cuts both in the number of beneficiaries and size of their benefits possible. Gilder and Murray indict all entitlement programs for the economic stagnation of the time, but disability compensation appeared guilty of the largest crime and was subject potentially to the most effective sentencing.

The election of Ronald Reagan in 1980 provided an opportunity for a partial trial of Murray's "thought experiment." Designed to unleash entrepreneurial activity, spur investment, and eliminate recourse to welfare programs, the Reagan revolution ultimately would be evaluated by its impact on the well-being of each of us as individuals and by its ability to revitalize the entire U.S. economy on the world stage. Entrepreneurs, unshackled, would benefit themselves, and in so doing benefit poor persons who would be newly employed and increasingly well remunerated by this enterprise. Again, Gilder (1981, 63) writes:

> It is the rich who by risking their wealth ultimately lose it, and save the economy. The risk-bearing role of the rich cannot be performed so well by anyone else. The benefits of capitalism still depend on capitalists. Under capitalism, when it is working, the rich have the anti-Midas touch, transforming timorous liquidity and unused savings into factories and office towers, farms and laboratories, orchestras and museums-turning gold into goods and jobs and art. That is the function of the rich: fostering opportunities for the classes below them in the continuing drama of the creation of wealth and progress.

Stripped of Gilder's purple prose, the Reagan Revolution had two parts: reduce the tax burdens upon the rich so that they would have more money available to build factories and hire workers, and eliminate welfare as an option for the poor because doing this would both allow tax rates to fall and ensure an adequate labor supply for those factories. In the long run this strategy would generate more wealth, allowing the wages of the poorest workers—indeed, of all workers—to rise, ironically generating more tax revenue for government along the way (Arthur Laffer's free lunch).

Both propositions proved false: reducing access to entitlement programs and lowering benefit levels did not alter the long-term trends in employment among persons with disabilities, and providing more money to the wealthy through reductions in taxes did not generate a rise in real incomes of workers.[3] Instead, the

[3]This chapter draws upon two sets of analyses. In the first, I analyze close to two decades of the National Health Interview Survey public use data tapes to establish employment trends in the population with and without disabilities. In the second, I collate government statistics drawn from a wide range of sources to chart changes in the scope of federal disability expenditures in particular and social welfare expenditures in general.

These two analyses are then joined to argue that disability compensation levels are not tied to labor force participation rates and that government expenditures and tax rates are not tied to more general well-being. In the text of the chapter, I use the longitudinal data on labor force participation rates, numbers of SSDI beneficiaries and levels of benefits, and national income and expenditure figures to make my case. These data show that when benefit levels were highest, so, too, were labor force participation rates among disabled workers and that real incomes were growing most quickly when

disabled had no recourse in the labor market and so when SSDI "reform" was instituted, they suffered a reduction in income. And the notion that the invisible hand provides guidance notwithstanding, money freed for entrepreneurship did not come with instructions, and the choices made did not bring real wages back to their early-1970s levels.

As the experience of other industrialized nations attests, managers have many options when faced with economic uncertainty. They can make new things of high value in new ways. They can make the same things more efficiently by investing in new technologies, and if successful, will employ the same number of workers, pay them more, and have lower unit labor costs. Or they can make old things in old ways, but by paying less for labor. All economies include a mix of these strategies, but during the last decade U.S. managers relied disproportionately on the last strategy. A new lexicon reflects this. Firms "downsize" or "rightsize" by "outplacing" or "displacing" workers. They wrest wage concessions from the remaining workers, sometimes by threatening to move or close factories. And then they "outsource" production to other firms, frequently offshore. Thus, we pursue retrenchment within the firm to match our retrenchment in the public sector. This chapter will demonstrate the effects of the strategy of retrenchment on individuals with and without disabilities, and on the economic well-being of the nation as a whole.

---

government expenditures rose the fastest. In the footnote material, I review the studies that use econometric modeling of individuals' decision to work to demonstrate that the relative level of wage versus entitlement income does not affect the labor force participation rate. I have relegated these studies to footnotes because of their technical nature and because the results are broadly consistent with the more direct findings reported here.

The conservative retort to arguments like those presented in this chapter is that entitlement cuts were not sufficient to have the intended effect on employment, and that true tax rates did not fall enough to spur investment. The data presented below, however, will indicate that SSDI entitlement rates and benefit levels did fall quite dramatically in the early 1980s (but to no avail with respect to labor force participation) and that tax burdens were lowered sufficiently among the wealthiest quintile of Americans to increase their share of income by about a fifth. Though this does not prove that shifting yet more income to the wealthy would not generate higher real incomes across the board in the long run, it does suggest it, and in any case it is hard to imagine that such redistribution ever could be sustained politically.

Labor Force Participation

No trend in U.S. society has been as well chronicled as the dramatic change in the labor force participation rates of women since World War II. This attention makes perfect sense, because women's entrance into the labor force had profound repercussions on the family and the market, as services formerly provided by women had to be procured elsewhere. Most analysts, however, focus on the overall trends in labor force participation among women of all working ages, obscuring important differences in employment patterns of women of different ages, and they omit mention of disturbing countertrends among men, especially nonwhite men. The initial surge of women into the labor force in the 1960s raised the proportion of all adults who work in quite dramatic fashion. During the last two decades, however, the increases among women have been partially offset by decreases among men, so that the overall labor force participation rate has risen slightly. Thus, the feminization of the labor force is part of the greater transformation from a manufacturing to a service economy. Chapters 4 and 5 explore these changes in greater detail. Here, I want to emphasize that the entrance of women has been accompanied by the exit of men and that older men and younger women have been disproportionately affected.

A Short History of Labor Market Dynamics

A little over four decades ago, Rosie the Riveter was sent home to take care of the children. Her husband's income allowed her to do so. In the 1950s, Frank Levy writes, median family income increased by over 40 percent and the average 30-year-old male wage earner had to pay only 14 percent of his gross income for his mortgage (Levy 1987). These rising incomes led, in turn, to large families, which, in reciprocal fashion, reinforced Rosie's decision to remain out of the labor force. The rapid increase in incomes continued almost without interruption during the 1960s (real incomes rose 3 percent a year during that decade). Nevertheless, some of the women who had raised children in the 1950s went back to work in the 1960s: labor force participation rates among women aged 55 to 64 rose from 37 percent to 43 percent during this decade (Table 3.1). The proportion of women of these ages who work has hardly risen since. While labor force participation among women in the immediate preretirement years has been relatively stagnant since 1970, rates among younger women have continued to climb, increasing during this time by a quarter among women aged 45–54, by more than 40 percent among women aged 18–44, and by a quarter across all working-age women. The social phenomenon of increasing participation in the labor force is largely concentrated among younger women. Many of these young women who work no doubt do so because more than fifteen years of declining real wages preclude families from living on the wages of a single worker, because of the increasing cost of living (the average mortgage on the average house now consumes over 40 percent of the average man's earnings), and because many of the women are raising children alone.

The decline in labor force participation among men is concentrated among those in the immediate preretirement years, having fallen by 20 percentage points among those aged 55 to 64 since 1960. This is not to deny the slight declines among men aged 45 to 54 and 18 to 44 (5 and 3 percentage points, respectively) or the steady erosion of employment opportunities for nonwhite men of all ages (see Figure 6.2 in Chapter 6). But it does indicate that in the aggregate, the largest portion of the overall decline in men's labor force participation occurred among those aged 55 to 64.

When older women began to enter the labor force during the 1960s, because of their small numbers, they did not have much of an impact on the overall labor force participation rate, increasing the proportion of adults working by a mere 2 percentage points between 1960 and 1970. The surge of young women entering the labor force during the 1970s, however, had profound repercussions, increasing the proportion of working-age adults in the labor force from 69 to 74 percent, or by more than 7 percent in relative terms. Although young women continued to enter the labor market during the 1980s, they did so at slower rates, barely replacing older men, fewer of whom now work than at any point in recent history. In truth, these women were not so much replacing men as taking on a different mix of occupations and industries than the ones formerly held by the men who had left work. The earlier phase of increasing participation among women represented net growth in employment (and prior to the mid-1970s, net growth at a time of rising real wages); the current phase is merely a shift in

Table 3.1. U.S. Labor Force Participation Rates of
the Working-Age Civilian Population by Sex and Age, 1960–1988 (percent of population)

Year	Both sexes, all ages	Males				Females			
		All ages	18–44	45–54	55–64	All ages	18–44	45–54	55–64
1960	67	93	94	96	87	43	42	50	37
1965	67	92	92	96	85	45	45	51	41
1970	69	90	91	94	83	50	51	55	43
1975	71	88	90	92	76	54	58	55	41
1980	74	88	91	91	72	61	66	60	41
1982	75	88	90	91	70	63	68	62	42
1985	76	88	91	91	68	65	71	64	42
1988	76	88	91	91	67	68	73	69	44

Sources: Author's analysis of data from U.S. Department of Labor 1961, 1971, 1981, 1986b, 1988a; U.S. Bureau of the Census 1984.

employment. As we shall see later in this chapter, this shift from older men to younger women has been accompanied by lower wages.[4]

The neoconservatives alleged that SSDI played a key role in allowing older men to withdraw from work. If so, the reforms instituted at the outset of the 1980s did not succeed, insofar as labor force participation rates among older men have continued to decline. The decline has been more precipitous among men with disabilities, the group for whom the reforms were designed. In 1970, the labor force participation rate among 55–64 year-old men with disabilities was about 60 percent of that among men of these ages without disabilities; the corresponding ratio has been about 48 percent in the last few years. In contrast, younger women with disabilities have entered the labor force only a bit more slowly than have young women in good health, which, I will argue later, reflects the demand for service, sales, and clerical workers in the 1980s.

The Social Security Disability Insurance Program

Legislative History

The SSDI program was initiated in 1056 to provide income to people who could no longer work because of illnesses expected to last into the future.[5] The program expanded upon a prior Social Security program to secure retirement benefits for those forced

[4]As I write this in 1991, the increase in the labor force participation rate seems to have ended a three-decade spurt, perhaps a temporary response to recession (U.S. Department of Labor 1991a). However, some speculate that the growth in service-related employment has reached a permanent end and that this reflects a saturation of the market for services rather than or at least in addition to, the effect of the economic downturn (Uchitelle 1991a; Nasar 1991a).

[5]The historiography of the SSDI program in particular and disability compensation programs in general is growing. Stein (1980) describes the origin of the SSDI program, albeit in a dry and almost exclusively chronological fashion. Berkowitz (1987) reviews the history of U.S. disability policy, his theme being the bias toward income replacement rather than rehabilitation. Stone (1984) and Derthick (1990) emphasize the politics of the SSDI Program, the former by demonstrating how the subjectivity inherent in disability evaluations results in a struggle between government and persons with disabilities to define the scope of benefits, and the latter by showing how inattention to administration allows disability politics to brew.

out of the labor market for health reasons. Unlike workers' compensation, which required that an illness or injury occur at work, or disabled veterans' pensions, which were granted only in the event of service-related disability, SSDI benefits were to be available to all those aged 50 or over who had been paying into the Social Security trust fund. In 1958 coverage was extended to dependents. In 1960 the age requirement was lifted, enabling younger individuals to qualify for benefits. Finally, in 1972 SSDI beneficiaries became eligible for Medicare benefits two years after first receiving entitlement to the program.

These programmatic changes were probably sufficient to spawn the growth that was to occur in the SSDI program, but they occurred as the prevalence of severe activity limitation increased at all ages,[6] as the overall population aged,[7] as the economy began to sputter, and as the first studies implicating SSDI in the decline of male labor force participation appeared.[8] As a result of these trends, the Carter administration proposed legislation, later adopted by Congress, to lower the absolute level of benefits and the proportion of one's working income that SSDI would replace.[9] This legislation also liberalized the benefits provided to SSDI beneficiaries during a trial work period in the hope that this would enable more of them to secure employment after a period of recovery. Finally, President Carter proposed more frequent and more stringent reviews of the entitlement of current beneficiaries, criteria that the Reagan administration implemented almost immediately after taking office.[10] These changes did more than stem the growth in the SSDI program; they reversed it.

But they did so at great political cost, and not at a propitious time. Hundreds of thousands of SSDI beneficiaries were removed from the rolls in 1981 and 1982 on the basis of administrative judgments that their conditions had improved, reviews whose findings were frequently incorrect and almost always easy to disprove if one hired a "physician expert" to testify (U.S. Congress 1984a, 1984b). Moreover, the purging came as the worst postwar

[6]See Verbrugge 1984.

[7]U.S. Bureau of the Census 1990.

[8]See, for example, Feldstein 1974.

[9]Berkowitz (1987, particularly chap. 4), recounts this legislative history.

[10]Derthick (1990) explores the implications of these changes for the administration of the SSDI program.

recession precluded even the healthy from finding work. As expected, the Democratic-controlled House held hearings to attack these changes; unexpectedly, the Republican-controlled Senate did so as well. As a result of the political backlash, the Reagan administration was forced to rescind the most egregious aspect of the new policy of periodic reviews: purging beneficiaries prior to a full hearing. This made removing people from the rolls far more difficult.

History of SSDI Entitlement

The process of establishing eligibility for disability benefit programs such as SSDI is fundamentally different from the process in other social welfare programs. To get benefits for most programs, one merely needs a birth certificate to prove age (as in the case of Social Security retirement benefits or Medicare) or an income statement to prove impoverishment (as in the case of Aid to Families with Dependent Children [AFDC] or food stamps). While the age of retirement for Social Security retirement benefits or the income level required for AFDC may be changed, proving eligibility remains a relatively simple process of verifying objective criteria.

In contrast, entitlement to disability benefits rests on judgments about individuals' capacity for work, judgments that can and do change with time. Some of these changes reflect improvements in medical treatment—lithium has turned some cases of manic-depressive illness into a short-term condition—and some reflect changes within work—computer assisted manufacturing has rendered many physically demanding jobs easier to do. But most reflect the political tenor of the times, alternate waves of resentment against those remunerated without having to work and against the heartless bureaucrats who would deny to the sick and infirm a just return on an insurance policy.[11]

Reflecting changing judgments about work capacity, the regulations underlying the SSDI have gone through several major revisions designed to reduce the probability that an application will result in entitlement, to reduce the size of the benefits, and to reduce the odds that once entitled, the individual will retain

[11]See Stone (1984) for a discussion of these issues. The entire book deals with these issues; therefore, I do not cite chapter and verse.

Table 3.2. Flow of Insured Population into and out of SSDI Beneficiary Pool, 1960–1988

Year	No. insured (millions)	Applications per 100,000 insured	Awards per 100,000 insured	Terminations per disabled beneficiary	Awards per application
1960	46.4	—[a]	448	.20	—
1965	53.3	993	476	.16	.48
1970	72.4	1,201	484	.18	.40
1975	83.3	1,542	711	.13	.46
1980	95.6	1,322	357	.14	.27
1982	102.4	997	290	.19	.29
1985	106.7	1,096	383	.13	.35
1988	115.3	800	358	.12	.45

Sources: Author's analysis of data from U.S. Department of Health and Human Services 1982, 3–14; id. 1985b, 199; id. 1986a, 226; id. 1986b, 34–37; 1987, 114, 131, 135, 232; id. 1989b, 148, 258, 262, 281.

[a]Dash indicates data not available.

benefits. Through a sometimes painful learning process, SSDI program administrators came to understand that some revisions are easier to sustain than others. It was much easier to reduce the number of applicants through changes in initial entitlement criteria than to terminate the benefits of those already receiving them. And it was easier to dissuade potential beneficiaries from applying than to deny applications already filed.

Table 3.2 charts the flow of beneficiaries into and out of the SSDI program since it was initiated, thus demonstrating this learning process within the SSDI bureaucracy. Applications first rose dramatically in the early 1970s, at their mid-decade peak reaching more than 1.5 percent of the insured population per year, but the rate at which benefits were awarded rose even faster. Thus, the probability of entitlement given an application (46 percent) was almost as high as it had been in 1965, when the program was still getting off the ground and when the application rate was more than a third lower. The Carter administration merely had to announce its intention to institute tougher entitlement standards to suppress the application rate, which dropped by 15 percent between 1975 and 1980, and to reduce the award rate by half.[12] The Reagan Administration, in contrast, actually instituted tougher regulations, causing the termination rate to increase by more than a third between 1980 and 1982. The termination rate has since fallen to its historical low, no doubt in response to the protests against the policy of terminating benefits prior to a hearing, proving that the threat of regulation is sometimes more effective than actual regulation. Since the award rate is rising again, albeit much more slowly than in the early 1970s, new regulations, or at least a hint of them, may be in the offing.

Reducing the number of new beneficiaries receiving entitlement and increasing the number of old beneficiaries purged from the rolls affects the stock of current beneficiaries, but at a lag. Figure 3.1 and Table 3.3 show the prevalence rates for disabled-worker beneficiaries and for all beneficiaries (disabled workers and their dependents); Table 3.3 also shows the raw counts for these groups over time. The application and award rates peaked in 1975, but the total numbers of disabled-worker and all beneficiaries were

[12]Parsons (1991) uses econometric analysis to show how changing eligibility criteria can suppress the application rate for SSDI.

Table 3.3. Number and Rate of SSDI Beneficiaries
by Type of Beneficiary, 1960–1988

Year	Disabled-worker beneficiaries		All beneficiaries	
	No.	Per 100,000 insured	No.	Per 100,000 population
1960	455,371	571	687,451	381
1965	988,074	1,854	1,739,051	900
1970	1,492,948	2,062	2,664,995	1,300
1975	2,488,774	2,047	4,352,200	2,015
1980	2,861,253	2,993	4,682,172	2,100
1982	2,603,713	1,796	3,973,465	1,709
1985	2,656,500	2,440	3,907,169	1,600
1988	2,830,284	2,496	4,074,300	1,659

Source: Author's analysis of data from U.S. Department of Health and Human Services 1985b, 93; id. 1986b, 37; id. 1989b, 148, 206; id. 1990b, 36, 56.

highest in 1980. At that point, the number of SSDI recipients approached 3 percent of the insured labor force, and the number of all beneficiaries, including dependents, exceeded 2 percent of the U.S. population, both rates having risen by about 50 percent in a decade. Between 1980 and 1982, the number of disabled-worker beneficiaries fell by 260,000; the number of disabled-worker beneficiaries per insured labor force participant fell by 13 percent. The number of dependents receiving SSDI benefits declined by 450,000 (datum not in table) and the number of all SSDI beneficiaries, including dependents, declined by more than 700,000 (17 percent in relative terms) during this time. This occurred while unemployment was reaching a thirty-year high. The confluence of severe recession and program retrenchment was a volatile mix politically, so it should come as no surprise that the regulations making the reductions in the SSDI rolls possible were partially rescinded.

As a result, since 1982 the number of disabled-worker beneficiaries has resumed its long-term rise, almost reaching its absolute peak in 1988 (the number per insured was still much lower than in 1980, and was remaining fairly constant). Because there are now fewer dependents per disabled-worker beneficiary, SSDI gradually has become more of what it was intended to be: com-

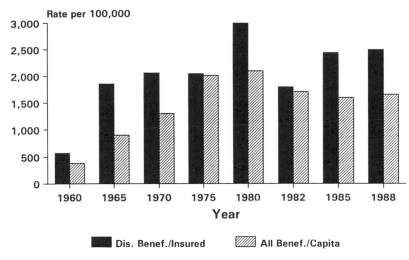

Fig. 3.1   Disabled-Worker and All Beneficiaries of SSDI, 1960–1988
Source: Author's calculations from U.S. Department of Health and Human Services
1990a, 51, 72; id. 1990b, 135.

pensation for those who cannot work because of illness, rather than a general income support program.

If statistics in general can be dry, program statistics are a desert. However, these data about the SSDI program tell a story of social welfare politics in the last three decades. Instituted incrementally in the 1950s and 1960s to avoid surveillance by business and legislators fearful of anything vaguely resembling national health insurance (Starr 1982; Berkowitz 1987, especially chap. 2), and then growing dramatically in the 1970s as employment problems first came to prominence, in the 1980s SSDI came to symbolize profligacy in government and malingering among individuals avoiding hard work when given the opportunity to do so. But the attempt to restrain SSDI backfired, allowing growth in the number of beneficiaries to resume. Charles Murray (1984) had tried to cast disability insurance in the same light as welfare. The public treated it, instead, as an insurance program, the benefits of which they were entitled to collect like those from any other form of annuity. Because of the popularity of the SSDI program and the unpopularity of the strategy of retrenchment, neither the Reagan nor the Bush administration attempted further "reforms." As with other social welfare issues, however, the bills of the 1980s are coming due, and the Bush administration will have to confront renewed program growth. If the program administrators learned anything from the experience of the early 1980s, they are unlikely to respond by terminating the benefits of those already receiving SSDI checks.

History of Benefit Levels

The politics of the SSDI program turn as much on the growth in the size of its benefits as in the number of beneficiaries. As the data in Chapter 2 indicate, one always can justify the increase in the magnitude of the beneficiary pool on the basis of demographic and health trends, forces seemingly beyond a policymaker's—or politician's—control. Benefit levels became an important issue during the 1970s because program expenditures depleted the disability trust fund, because SSDI benefits began to take a sizable portion of the federal social budget, potentially undermining other worthwhile programs, and because the amount of a monthly check can be revised. Program analysts worried about both the absolute level program expenditures had reached and the impact of their rise relative to other, less remunerative forms of social welfare and to work. They were especially concerned about the magnitude of new awards (benefit levels among newly entitled recipients), since these were rising while real wages—the alternative for those deciding whether to persevere at work in the face of illness—declined.

Rising benefit levels are inherent in all Social Security programs, both because they reflect the higher earnings and longer coverage of successive cohorts of workers and because in recent years, Social Security checks have risen in tandem with the Consumer Price Index.[13] Thus, newly entitled SSDI beneficiaries received 12 percent more in 1970 than in 1960 ($397 versus $354 in 1988 terms); Table 3.4 presents data on average SSDI benefits among all beneficiaries and among those newly receiving entitlement over time. During the 1970s, however, the magnitude of awards to newly disabled workers increased by a third, average benefits among all disabled workers increased by 40 percent, and average benefits among all beneficiaries, including dependents, increased by 37 percent. These figures underestimate the true increase in the value of the SSDI benefits. After 1972, SSDI recip-

[13]U.S. Department of Health and Human Services 1989b.

Table 3.4. Average Monthly SSDI Award and Benefit Level for Disabled Workers and All Beneficiaries, 1960–1988 (1988 Dollars)

Year	Average awards, disabled workers[a]	Average benefits, disabled workers	Average benefits, all beneficiaries
1960	354	279	362
1965	366	261	366
1970	397	276	424
1975	495	342	528
1980	531	386	581
1982	538	406	542
1985	528	340	517
1988	530	413	538

Sources: U.S. Department of Health and Human Services 1986b 37–38, 58; id. 1990b, 36–37, 58; U.S. Bureau of the Census 1988, 450.

[a]The term award means the level of benefits among persons who are newly entitled to SSDI. See U.S. Department of Health and Human Services 1989b, 356.

ients became eligible for Medicare two years after their first SSDI benefits were awarded. This proved especially valuable to those for whom the alternative was either Medicaid (which fewer physicians accept) or an expensive private policy. Indeed, most SSDI beneficiaries had been unable to purchase private health insurance prior to the enactment of this legislation, ironically because of the "preexisting" conditions that had entitled them to SSDI in the first place.

The 1980 reforms stabilized benefit levels throughout the ensuing decade. SSDI awards among newly disabled workers were no higher in 1988 than they had been in 1980. Average benefits among all disabled workers were only a little higher in 1988 (having fallen dramatically in the interim before regaining lost ground), while average benefits among all beneficiaries fell, reflecting attempts to reconstitute SSDI as a program for disabled workers, not all citizens. Since the preponderance of program costs derive from benefits paid to disabled workers and the number of such beneficiaries and the magnitude of their monthly checks are rising again, the reforms in the 1980s may have provided only a severe downward ratchet in the program, albeit one that removed seven hundred thousand people from the rolls and temporarily decreased the incomes of the remaining beneficiaries,

Table 3.5. Average Monthly U.S. Transfer Payments by Program and Type of Beneficiary, 1960–1988 (1988 dollars)

Year	SSI Average SSI payment, all states, all entitlements	SSI Average SSI payment, all states, disabled beneficiaries	AFDC Average payment for individuals	AFDC Average payment for families	Disabled veterans Average payment to beneficiaries, including dependents	Black Lung Average payment to beneficiaries, including dependents
1960			110	415		
1965			118	488	265	
1970			144	546	283	247
1975	243	309	147	473	308	354
1980	239	281	135	393	315	302
1982	239	278	124	363	333	303
1985	250	287	126	373	336	316
1988	260	294	129	375		304

Source: Author's analysis of data from U.S. Department of Health and Human Services, 1985b, 242, 230; 1986b, 48; 1989b, U.S. Bureau of the Census, 1983b.

in the process lowering the base from which future cost-of-living increases will be computed.[14]

The Microeconomic Context of SSDI Benefits

SSDI is an alternative to work—and with rising benefit levels, an increasingly attractive one. But it is also an alternative to other disability programs for which the potential SSDI beneficiary might qualify, as well as such means-tested programs as SSI and welfare. Thus, SSDI stands indicted for enticing those in the labor force to stop work and for enticing potential beneficiaries of other entitlement programs—which pay less—to apply for SSDI benefits. Table 3.5 shows how benefits in these other programs have changed through time.

The principal non-means-tested national disability programs include Black Lung benefits, instituted in 1970 to compensate coal miners with pulmonary conditions arising from work[15] and disabled veterans' pensions which compensate those with military service-connected impairments (Burkhauser and Haveman 1982). Benefits paid to Black Lung program beneficiaries and their dependents rose substantially in the early 1970s, reaching a peak of $354 a month (in 1988 terms) in 1975. Since then, the value of these benefits has fallen by about 15 percent, and they pay less than 60 percent as much as the SSDI program. Disabled veterans' pensions fared a little better, but they have never paid more than about two-thirds as much as the SSDI program.

First instituted in the mid-1970s to replace separate programs for the aged, poor, blind, and disabled, Supplemental Security Income (SSI) is the principal income support for disabled individuals whose employment histories are not sufficient to qualify them for SSDI (U.S. Department of Health and Human Services,

[14]The appearance of stasis in benefit levels may be deceiving insofar as current beneficiaries had higher earnings histories (and paid far higher premiums) than did those from a decade ago; yet they are receiving checks of the same relative magnitude. They are no doubt receiving a smaller return on the SSDI portion of Social Security taxes they paid than did earlier beneficiaries.

[15]For the history of this program, particularly of how political considerations defined pulmonological impairment as a disease, see Fox and Stone (1980). Fox and Stone portray the growth of the Black Lung program as stemming from the decline of the coal industry, thus tying disability compensation to industrial change in this one case study in a manner consistent with my thesis.

Table 3.6. Average Annual Personal Income, Wages and Salaries, and
SSDI Awards, 1950–1988 (1988 Dollars)

Year	Personal income per capita	Wages and salaries per labor force participant	SSDI awards per recipient
1950	7,255	11,275	
1960	8,790	15,018	4,316
1965	10,447	18,024	4,316
1970	11,921	19,480	5,056
1973	13,209	20,857	6,288
1975	13,244	17,178	6,296
1980	13,494	17,743	6,917
1982	13,899	17,415	5,861
1985	15,237	18,487	6,257
1988	16,500	19,688	6,457

Source: Author's analysis of data from the U.S. Bureau of the Census, 1983b, 6, 405; id. 1986, 8, 421; U.S. Department of Health and Human Services 1985b, 66; id. 1989b, 99; id. 1990b, 56.

1989b). SSI benefits for the disabled have always been just slightly over one-half of SSDI, amounting to $294 in 1988. Thus, SSDI pays monthly benefits from 40 to 100 percent more than those of other disability compensation programs, and the gap is at least as big as it has ever been.

Although persons with chronic conditions would rarely draw upon a nondisability income-support program, such as AFDC, I have noted the average benefit levels for this program (in Table 3.5) to indicate how much better persons receiving SSDI benefits have fared. While the average benefits of disabled-worker beneficiaries were as high as they had ever been in 1988, AFDC benefits have declined steadily since 1970, the value of payments to individuals having fallen by 10 percent and that of payments to families by a third during this time. Thus, the United States has established a hierarchy of income-support programs: persons with disabilities who meet the SSDI eligibility criteria are better supported than persons with disabilities who do not, and both groups are better supported than clients of nondisability programs. Although the value of SSDI benefits stabilized during the 1980s, their value relative to other income-support programs continued to be high. The same cannot be said about the value of SSDI benefits relative to real wages.

Table 3.7. Average U.S. Hourly and Weekly Wages and Average Number of Hours Worked per Week, 1950–1988

Year	Average hourly wages	Average weekly wages (1988 Dollars)	Average hours worked per week
1950	6.45	255	39.5
1960	8.18	317	38.8
1965	9.04	353	39.1
1970	9.65	359	37.2
1975	9.78	354	36.2
1980	9.36	330	35.3
1982	9.21	320	34.8
1985	9.34	326	34.9
1988	9.29	322	34.7

Sources: Author's analysis of data from U.S. Department of Labor 1985b, 194, 201; id. 1990a, 84–87.

When the first energy crisis hit in 1973, the real wages of workers started to fall. Even after a period of recovery in the mid- and late 1980s, 1988 real wages were, depending on the measure chosen, either substantially below the early 1970s peak or just approaching their peak levels. Table 3.6 shows the changes in personal income and in wages and salaries over time; Table 3.7 breaks the change in wages and salaries down into changes in hourly and weekly wages and hours worked each week. For example, in 1973 wages and salary disbursements were just under $21,000 per year in 1988 terms (Table 3.6). In the ensuing decade, they fell by as much as 20 percent, before regaining some of this lost ground. Even in 1988, however, they remained 6 percent lower than they had been in 1973. Meanwhile, average hourly wages declined by about 5 percent from their early 1970s peak, and average weekly earnings declined by about 10 percent, primarily because the work week had become shorter (Table 3.7). Other measures of compensation also reveal a pattern of decline (Table 3.8).[16] Given the exceptional growth in real wages

[16]Table 3.8 shows the change in the Employment Cost Index (ECI), the Bureau of Labor Statistics (BLS) measure of change, for wages and salaries and for total compensation, including benefits paid by employers to personnel; the measure excludes farm workers, household employees, and the self-

Table 3.8. U.S. Employment Cost Index (ECI) and Consumer Price Index
(CPI), 1981–1988

| | ECI | | | | CPI |
| | Wages and salaries | | Total compensation | | |
Year	Index	% Change	Index	% Change	% Change
1981	103.8		104.0		
1982	110.3	6.3	110.7	6.4	6.2
1983	115.8	5.0	117.0	5.6	3.2
1984	120.6	4.1	122.7	4.9	4.2
1985	125.6	4.1	127.5	3.9	3.6
1986	129.5	3.1	131.6	3.2	1.9
1987	133.8	3.3	136.0	3.3	3.6
1988	139.3	4.1	142.6	4.9	4.1
Total		34.2		37.1	30.0

Source: Author's analysis of data from the U.S. Department of Labor 1983, 1984,
1985a, 1986a, 1987, 1990a; U.S. Department of Health and Human Services, 1990a.

throughout the 1950s and 1960s, there is no doubt that—whatever
the measure—real wages are much below what we had come to
expect they would be as the 1970s began.

Paradoxically, per capita income has been rising for the fifteen
years that real wages have been relatively stagnant (Table 3.6).
This is because nonwage income (transfers, including Social Security and welfare, as well as interest and dividends) increased by
about 17 percent since 1970. Workers have been financing these
gains.

As part of the increase in nonwage income, SSDI awards rose by
about 30 percent, even taking the post-1980 drop into account
(Figure 3.2). In 1980, someone newly entitled to SSDI benefits
received 39 percent as much as the typical worker and about one-

---

employed. The BLS has calculated the total compensation measure only since
1981. Wages and salaries increased about 34 percent during this time, and
total compensation increased by 37 percent, principally because health insurance costs have been rising rapidly. The ECI does not reflect change in real
earnings among individual workers, however, since this index measures the
total cost of compensation for all workers, not the cost of compensating a
worker. A large component of employer cost growth was due to the growth in
the number of workers hired and growth in the magnitude of payments for
health insurance, rather than to rising real wages.

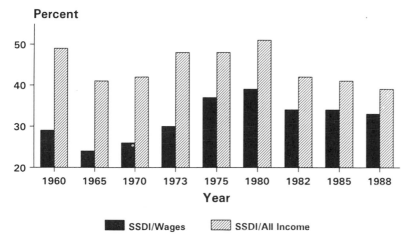

Fig. 3.2   Ratio of SSDI Benefits to Wages and All Income, 1960–1988
Source: Author's calculations from U.S. Department of Health and Human Services 1990a, 51, 72; id. 1990b, 135.

half of per capita income—more when the tax benefits of lower gross income and the value of Medicare are taken into account. In contrast, real wages rose much more quickly during the 1960s. During this time, SSDI awards amounted to only about one-quarter of the typical worker's income.

Until the recent reforms in Social Security, almost all of each year's expenditures derived from that year's payroll taxes. Thus, workers whose own incomes were falling financed substantial increases in the standard of living of SSDI beneficiaries. Some suggest that SSDI awards approaching 40 percent of wages enticed a large number of workers to leave employment, further exacerbating the burden this program placed on those still in the labor force.

Of course, workers also financed increases in Social Security retirement benefits (over 60 percent between 1970 and 1988). And with the tax cuts in the early 1980s, they witnessed even larger increases in interest payments (about 70 percent). As a result, the share of national income accruing to workers fell by 10 percent, while nonwage income increased by a fifth during this time. Net of declines in means-tested income programs and proprietor's income, nonwage income grew by more than 40 percent in relative terms. Despite this tremendous transfer of wealth from the

Table 3.9. GNP, Total Federal Expenditures, Total Federal Social Expenditures, and SSDI Program Expenditures, 1950–1988

Year	GNP[a]	Federal expenditures		Federal social expenditures			SSDI expenditures			
		Total	% of GNP	Total	% of GNP	% of Federal expenditures	Total	% of GNP	% of Federal Social expenditures	% of Federal expenditures
1950	286.5	42.6	14.9	10.5	3.7	24.7				
1960	506.5	92.2	18.2	25.0	4.9	27.1	0.53	0.001	0.021	0.006
1965	673.6	118.2	17.6	37.7	5.6	31.9	1.39	0.002	0.037	.012
1970	992.7	195.7	19.7	77.3	7.8	39.5	2.78	0.003	0.036	.014
1975	1,598.4	332.3	20.8	167.4	10.5	50.4	7.63	0.005	0.046	.023
1980	2,631.7	590.9	22.5	302.6	11.5	51.2	14.89	0.006	0.049	.025
1982	3,166.0	745.7	23.6	367.7	11.6	49.3	17.40	0.006	0.047	.023
1985	4,010.3	946.3	23.6	451.2	11.3	47.7	18.65	0.005	0.047	.020
1987	4,524.3	1,004.6	22.2	499.8	11.0	49.8	20.50	0.005	0.041	.020
1988	4,880.6	1,064.0	21.8	533.3	10.9	50.1	21.39	0.004	0.040	0.020

Source: Author's analysis of data from the U.S. Bureau of the Census 1975, 433; id. 1977, 432, 433; id. 1986, 305, 354, 431; id. 1990, 7, 378, 432; U.S. Department of Health and Human Services 1986b, 31; 1989, 130.

[a]GNP, Federal expenditures, Federal social expenditures, and SSDI expenditures expressed in billions of dollars.

working to the nonworking population and despite the important part Social Security played in this dynamic, SSDI and Social Security remain very popular programs. If the neoconservatives were selling the argument that entitlement was to blame for economic stagnation, the public refused to buy it.

The Macroeconomic Context of the SSDI Program

The cost of the SSDI program is a function of the number of beneficiaries and the magnitude of their benefits. The number of SSDI beneficiaries peaked around 1980 (Table 3.3), as did average benefits across all beneficiaries (Table 3.4), at which point SSDI expenditures consumed about 0.6 percent of the gross national product (GNP). Table 3.9 charts the change in the federal portion of GNP, in federal social expenditures, and in SSDI expenditures over time. During the 1960s SSDI grew threefold in real terms, and it doubled in the 1970s. The growth in the earlier decade, however, was a result of the initiation of the program. The growth in the 1970s reflected a more complex set of dynamics, including, depending on one's point of view, increased income replacement rates, declining will to work, more liberal interpretation of entitlement criteria, or the aging of the population. After the reforms of the 1980s, expenditures for SSDI declined by a third in relative terms. Since the number of beneficiaries and the average level of their benefits are growing again, however, these may be one-time savings.

The growth in the SSDI program prior to 1980 occurred in the context of a dramatically expanding federal role in the economy. Between 1950 and 1980, federal expenditures grew by one-half in real terms (to almost 23 percent of GNP), while federal social expenditures more than tripled (from less than 4 to more than 11 percent of GNP). Since then, substantial relative declines in SSDI (from 0.6 to 0.4 percent of GNP) and in all federal social expenditures (from 11.5 to 10.9 percent of GNP, a decline of 5 percent) have occurred. During the early part of the 1980s, the federal share of GNP increased, while federal social expenditures and SSDI were in decline. Thus, the social budget in general and SSDI expenditures in particular financed substantial growth in debt service (60 percent as of 1985) and the military budget (24 percent in real terms).

These transfers might be stated in more personal terms. The real wages of military personnel changed little between 1980 and 1985, but military contracts for the private sector grew from $87 billion to $140 billion (in 1985 terms). Likewise, the rising levels of interest income noted above at least in part reflect the relative growth in federal deficits. Thus, incomes derived from the federal budget were transferred from the recipients of social wages to the employees and stockholders of military contractors and individuals holding federal notes (including many foreigners). While many of the recipients of social wages are not poor, many are. On the other hand, the people benefiting from the growth in military contracts and government debt are almost never poor. As a result of these shifts due to changes in the federal budget and of the declining real wages noted above, the distribution of incomes is much less equal than it was as the 1980s began. The income share of the poorest quintile of families declined by a tenth (from 5.1 to 4.6 percent), and the share of the richest quintile rose by about 6 percent during this time. The wealthiest 5 percent of families experienced a 12 percent increase in their share of aggregate income between 1980 and 1988.[17]

Some of these dynamics have changed a little in the interim. The federal share of GNP declined somewhat in the latter part of the decade, primarily because of a slowdown in military expenditures and a slight reduction in the magnitude of the federal debt. As a result, the federal social budget has risen relative to the remainder of federal expenditures, even as the proportion of GNP going to the social budget continues its decline. The recipients of social largesse are getting a larger slice of the smaller federal pie. They are more likely to notice that they are eating less pie, however. Meanwhile, SSDI recipients continue to finance other people, their share of federal social expenditures having fallen by 18 percent and their share of all federal expenditures by 20 percent during the 1980s (as noted above, their share of GNP declined by a third).

In a time in which wage earners and recipients of social programs transferred huge sums of money to military contractors and holders of debt, not all did so equally. Recipients of Social Security retirement benefits fared the best, sustaining neither cuts in the number of beneficiaries nor cuts in the value of benefits.

[17]See Levy 1987; Phillips 1990; and U.S. Bureau of the Census 1987, 1988.

Recipients of means-tested income programs fared the worst, suffering losses of as much as one-half the value of their benefits. Wage earners and recipients of SSDI fall somewhere in between. Within the SSDI program itself, the number of dependents relative to disabled-worker beneficiaries receiving SSDI fell. And the value of newly awarded benefits relative to average benefits among all disabled-worker beneficiaries declined. Thus, younger workers and dependents bore a disproportionate share of the retrenchment in the SSDI program.

Summary

The academic theory that rising relative benefit levels account for rising disability rates underlay the efforts, ultimately successful, to reduce the number of disability beneficiaries and the size of their incomes. An examination of program statistics and national income accounts—the most neutral, and perhaps lifeless way, our society has devised of portraying someone's plight—provides a test of this theory.

Murray (1984) described the national agenda for disability compensation accurately when he wrote about cutting the knot. And cut the knot we did. Between 1980 and 1982 alone, the termination rate for SSDI beneficiaries increased by 35 percent, the number of disabled-worker beneficiaries per insured worker decreased by 13 percent and the number of all beneficiaries per capita decreased by 17 percent, and the replacement rate (ratio of SSDI awards to income) was reduced by almost 20 percent. These cuts recast SSDI from a program of general income support to one more narrowly focused on disability compensation for severely disabled workers alone.

This strike at the SSDI program, designed as part of the larger strategy of providing fewer alternatives to work, had no effect whatsoever on the labor force participation of persons with disabilities. Indeed, labor force participation rates among such persons have continued to fall throughout this period. Consequently, while there are more persons with disabilities, fewer work and fewer yet have access to SSDI benefits. Victims of a cruel paradox, persons with disabilities, whose numbers are increasing, have seen reductions in the SSDI program, their principal source of income. Because SSDI could be cut, it was.

In retrospect, we can see the folly of the notion that the growth in the SSDI program was due to malingering.[18] To receive SSDI benefits, one must have a condition expected to last two years and be out of work six months before applying. At that point, one has less than a 50 percent chance of succeeding in getting benefits. The proportion of applicants who succeeded in getting SSDI benefits has been as low as a quarter this past decade. If one does manage to get benefits, they will total just slightly more than $6,000 a year, about a third of average wages. This assumes one understands the application process, the chance of getting benefits, and the magnitude of awards prior to leaving work. It would not be surprising if this were a gamble few of us would take. And it should not be surprising that a policy predicated on this kind of behavior failed to reduce the work disability rate.

The demographic-medical need model of work disability rests on the notion that the presence of disease necessitates the withdrawal from work, a notion easy to refute with data showing that persons with disabilities were once able to keep working in very physically demanding jobs. The economic model of work disability rests on the notion that individuals equilibrate work and leisure by calculating the ratio of working and nonworking incomes, a notion easy to refute with the observation that lower ratios did not result in higher work rates. In the chapters that follow, I sketch a new model of work disability, tying the work disability rate to the transformation from a manufacturing to a service economy.

[18]By malingering, I mean choosing disability rather than work when work is physically possible. By arguing that there is no statistical basis to the claim that persons with disabilities malinger, I do not intend to state that individuals never malinger, just that one cannot associate labor force decisions with the choice between working and nonworking incomes in a systematic fashion (Yelin 1986).

4

Neither All Good nor All Bad but Definitely Different: The Transformation of the Labor Force, 1970–1990

Putting a spin on labor market trends is a growth industry.[1] Some view these trends as evidence of proletarianization of the work force and erosion of U.S. dominance in the world economy. Others see them as the inevitable consequence of positive economic and social developments, the former due to the growth of services

[1] In putting my own spin on labor market trends, I have been helped by two remarkable books, Paul Osterman's (1988) *Employment Futures: Reorganization, Dislocation, and Public Policy* and Frank Levy's (1987) *Dollars and Dreams: The Changing American Income Distribution.* Osterman describes how the internal labor market of the firm meshed well with the industrial manufacturing system of the first twenty-five years after World War II, but then unraveled when U.S. manufacturing failed to meet the challenges posed by the first energy crisis in 1973. Levy ties the changes in the macroeconomic environment to the lives of typical Americans at various points of the income distribution. These two volumes together give a comprehensive picture of how the world and national economy impinge on the day-to-day operation of the workplace and the day-to-day well-being of the family, in effect, covering the impact of macroeconomic changes on each part of daily life.

The data in need of a spin derive from my own analysis of the employment questions in the National Health Interview Survey and federal labor market data published in the *Monthly Labor Review,* the annual *Statistical Abstract of the United States,* and two compendia of data, *Labor Force Statistics Derived from the Current Population Survey, 1948–1987* (U.S. Department of Labor 1988b) and *Handbook of Labor Statistics* (U.S. Department of Labor 1985b). Richard Belous's (1989) *The Contingent Economy: The Growth of the Temporary, Part-Time and Subcontracted Workforce* is the source of the data on various categories of contingent labor. Finally, Blank (1990) uses the same data source and comes to much the same conclusion about the magnitude and cause of the growth in part-time employment.

at manufacturing's expense, the latter as jobs take a smaller physical toll from workers. This contentious debate merely continues one begun nearly two decades ago with the publication of Daniel Bell's (1973) influential book, *The Coming of Post-Industrial Society: A Venture in Social Forecasting.*

Bell popularized the term post-industrialism, using it both to summarize the changes then occurring in the U.S. society, and to forecast the shape of that society were those changes to continue.[2] Most people interpret the term literally and narrowly as a shift away from brute force production of tangible items. But Bell meant much more than this, and much less. In moving away from old forms of industrialism, the basis of society would change as well, with theoretical knowledge, flexibility, and cooperation replacing empirical knowledge, relatively fixed modes of production, and intense competition, and with the culture coming to reflect this change in orientation. This was the more of post-industrialism. The less is that society would still be geared toward production, indeed, production of material things. However, raw inputs of labor, material, and capital would cease to be the primary source of productivity growth. In the economic sphere, such intangibles as social organization and theoretical knowledge would drive production. We would still be producing tangible items—the basis of industrialism would remain intact—but the sources of industrialism would be post-industrial in nature.

Post-industrialism can not be observed directly, but we know it's there by watching such signposts as the shift from a goods-producing to a service-producing economy, the shift from producer to consumer goods, the shift from manufacturing occupations to professional and technical ones, and the shift in the culture of the economy from rigid production based on time-honored recipes to flexible production based on changes in social organization. We might still be making cars, but we will do so in fundamentally different ways. Industrialism means take a ton of steel, a thousand kilowatts of power, and fifty hours of labor and repeat six million times until retooling allows us to change models next year. Post-industrialism means responding to yester-

---

[2]He did not invent the term *post-industrialism,* however. Touraine's (1971) *The Post-Industrial Society,* published two years earlier, postulated that education and social organization were probably main elements of "the residual" category responsible for the much of productivity growth in the modern era.

day's rise in the price of oil on the futures market by shifting to production of high mileage models today (retooling on the fly) and by reorganizing the shop floor to cut the time to shift production from large to smaller models. In industrialism, increasing technology meant changing the mix of physical inputs to lower the cost and then generating the market for the cars as an afterthought. If the market eroded, production stopped altogether. In post-industrial production, there is a much quicker and subtler response to market signals, and the response is as likely to be organizational as technical.

Many of the trends Bell placed at the center of post-industrialism were not new ones when he wrote, but they were accelerating. The nature of manufacturing had already evolved several times in the last century, as craft-based production had given way to mass production based on human power, then steam, and subsequently electricity.[3] Indeed, one might argue that the major catalyst for this evolution had been the social organization of production advocated by Frederick Taylor ([1911] 1967) in his *Principles of Scientific Management,* rather than the development of more sophisticated ways of applying physical power to work. The emphasis on consumer products had been in place since at least the 1920s, when the auto and electronic industries first flowered.[4] The source of productivity growth had long ago ceased to be physical inputs, and it had been already been two decades since economists began to recognize this startling fact.[5]

Moreover, the post-industrial society would not emerge just because each of these trends might continue unabated. Social organization is the glue that ties the various trends together in meaningful and productive ways. Bell warned that the failure of

[3]This argument was shaped by David Noble's (1986) *The Forces of Production: A Social History of Industrial Automation,* which recounts these changes in industrial processes, but notes that the desire for control on the shop floor dictated the technology at least as much as the reverse.

[4]Many analysts emphasize the importance of the 1920s because it was during this decade that the production of consumer products took off, giving rise in turn to national marketing networks, chain stores, and advertising, all of the latter requiring more intense forms of managerial integration. See, for example, Wiebe 1967; Weinstein 1968; Chandler 1977, 1990; and Hirschhorn 1974.

[5]See Solow's (1957) seminal paper, "Technical Change and the Aggregate Production Function."

social institutions to overcome the atomistic tendencies of our society would thwart the development of post-industrialism, turning each positive trend into a nightmare. Absent the glue, the shift from production of goods to services might mean substitution of consumption now for production later and of high-wage manufacturing jobs for low-wage service work. Absent the glue, technical information would be hoarded or used for purposes of social control, rather than fueling economic development. Finally, absent the glue, post-industrialism might mean deskilling of jobs and unemployment as automation proceeded.

Soon after Bell wrote *The Coming of Post-Industrial Society,* Alan Gartner and Frank Riessman (1974) published a rejoinder arguing that Bell read too much into disparate trends and warning that the kind of services that were growing were low-level ones for individuals, not high-level ones fostering the productivity of manufacturing. Harry Braverman (1974) expanded upon this theme in his influential book, *Labor and Monopoly Capital.* Braverman warned that the technologies of the economy would render increasing proportions of the labor force powerless because automation both erodes the skill content of work—including white-collar work—and slackens the demand for labor.[6]

Twenty years later, we are still debating on Bell's terms, trying to decide if post-industrialism exists (is the mix of goods and services produced evidence of post-industrialism?) or even if it should (can wealth be generated when manufacturing withers?), and then arguing about the implications of the changes in the labor market for individuals (are jobs getting better or worse?) and for the economy as a whole (have these changes in work helped or hurt?).

The next two chapters describe the transformation in employment since 1970, this one focusing on quantifiable characteristics of jobs and Chapter 5 emphasizing changes in how work is done and in how it might be done. In doing so, the chapters provide the data that form the grist for the labor market analysts' mills, but my purpose is not to resolve the debate between the camps so much as to emphasize that the objective conditions of work have

[6]The argument that much white-collar work can be routinized, especially that of paper shufflers in the public and private bureaucracies, is generally associated with the French sociologist Serge Mallet (1975). See also Edwards 1979.

changed in such fundamental ways that we need a new map to understand them. Some of the changes are obvious. The manufacturing sector employs a much smaller proportion of workers, the service sector a much greater one. In turn, the demand for service and sales workers and managers has soared, while craft workers, operatives, and laborers have suffered displacement from jobs many had held for decades. It is also obvious to most of us that the terms of employment are different now, with fewer workers in full-time jobs with benefits and pay to match, and with the demand for unskilled labor slack. Most people associate the acceleration of displacement and the growth in contingent work with the shift from manufacturing to services, but these changes occurred in all industries and occupations. Increasingly, labor became another part of just-in-time inventory, brought in on a temporary or part-time basis and on a moment's notice when demand increased, laid off immediately thereafter.

I will try to be agnostic in describing these changes; my goal is to demonstrate that the kinds of jobs and the terms of employment are radically different from those that existed in 1970, rather than to label the changes. I say *try* because it is hard to remain agnostic when wages stagnate for close to two decades, when fewer workers report secure and adequately romunerated employment, and when jobs migrate from those who need them the most. However, the changes are fact and whether they are good for General Motors or not, or good for the nation or not, they change the composition of the labor force and the nature of the employment contract. I note them here because they create a poor climate in which to maintain or secure jobs for workers with disabilities. Thus, my goal in this and the subsequent chapter is to demonstrate that the weather is changing. In Chapter 6, I will show that the rain that fell over all workers became torrential when it hit those with disabilities.

The Work We Do and Where We Do It

For love or money more people are in the labor force than ever before; the size of the labor force has been rising in both absolute and relative terms since the early 1970s (excluding the periods of recession), exceeding population growth by wide margins.

Table 4.1. U.S. Employment Levels by Industry, 1970, 1982, and 1987

Industry Classification	1970		1982		1987		Change								
							1970–1982			1982–1987			1970–1987		
	No.	%	No.	%	No.	%	Abs.	Rel.	Share	Abs.	Rel.	Share	Abs.	Rel.	Share
Agricultural, fisheries, mining	3.16	4.1	4.16	4.0	4.04	3.5	1.00	31.6	-2.4	-0.12	-2.9	-12.5	0.88	27.9	-14.6
Construction	5.18	6.7	6.22	6.0	7.58	6.6	1.04	20.1	-10.5	1.36	21.9	10.0	2.40	46.3	-1.5
Manufacturing	19.98	25.7	23.50	22.6	22.66	19.8	3.52	11.8	-12.1	-0.84	-3.6	-12.4	2.68	13.4	-15.7
Transportation, communications, utilities	5.31	6.8	7.01	6.8	8.09	7.1	1.70	32.3	0.0	1.08	15.4	4.4	2.78	52.4	4.4
Wholesale/retail	14.70	18.9	19.44	18.8	21.34	18.7	4.74	32.3	-0.5	1.90	9.8	-0.5	6.64	45.2	-1.1
Finance, insurance, real estate	3.93	5.1	6.22	6.0	7.57	6.6	2.29	58.3	17.6	1.35	21.7	10.0	3.64	92.6	29.4
Services	19.93	25.6	29.53	28.4	34.74	30.4	10.78	48.2	10.9	5.21	17.6	7.0	14.81	74.3	18.8
Government	4.49	5.8	6.03	5.8	5.39	4.7	1.54	34.3	0.0	-0.64	-10.6	-19.0	0.90	20.0	-19.0
Total	77.82		103.91		114.38		26.09	33.5		10.47	10.1		36.56	47.0	

Source: Author's analysis of 1970, 1982, and 1987 National Health Interview Survey data.

Notes: No. = millions of workers; % = percent of total labor force in a specified year; abs. = absolute difference between years; rel. = percent change between years; share = percent change in percent of total labor force between years. Totals for numbers of persons and percentages of labor force do not equal sum of cells in columns because of omission of those whose industry was unknown and because of rounding.

Principally because younger women have entered jobs faster than older men have left them, the proportion of the working-age population in the labor force has risen by more than 10 percent since 1970 (the absolute number of people in the labor force has increased by 47 percent).[7]

A shift in the share of employment among industries and occupations accompanied this increased penetration. Tables 4.1 and 4.2 chart these shifts for industries and occupations, respectively. The tables show the absolute number of workers in an industry (or occupation) and the proportion of all workers in that industry (or occupation) for each of three years: 1970, just before the stagflation of the 1970s began; 1982, the nadir of the most serious recession in the last fifty years; and 1987, the end of an unprecedented period of employment growth. The tables also show absolute and relative change in the number of workers in an industry (or occupation), and change in that industry's (or occupation's) share of total employment.

Because of the magnitude of the overall growth in jobs, no industry employed fewer workers in 1987 than in 1970 (Table 4.1). Even in manufacturing, the absolute number of workers grew by more than two million (13.4 percent) during this time. Absolute employment also expanded in every industry between 1970 and 1982. In that sense, hiring exceeded displacement in every sector of the economy over the long haul. The jobs might be located in different firms, different sites within metropolitan areas or states, or different regions, but real jobs were being created in every industry, far more than were destroyed. Thus, deindustrialization (meaning demanufacturing) involves loss of share, not absolute decline.[8]

Manufacturing's share of employment eroded steadily throughout the seventeen years under study, comprising more than a

---

[7]U.S. Bureau of the Census 1990, 378.

[8]Bluestone and Harrison (1982) coined the term *deindustrialization*, but they, too, meant it in relative, not absolute terms. On the other hand, they warned that deindustrialization had become something of an economic strategy among companies who were transferring manufacturing activities out of the industrial belt, indeed, out of the country, and who were also making the transition from manufacturing to services because of the squeeze on profits in manufacturing activities and the favorable tax treatment accorded service industries.

Table 4.2. U.S. Employment Levels by Occupation, 1970, 1982, and 1987

Occupation	1970 No.	1970 %	1982 No.	1982 %	1987 No.	1987 %	Change 1970–1982 Abs.	Rel.	Share	Change 1982–1987 Abs.	Rel.	Share	Change 1970–1987 Abs.	Rel.	Share
Professionals	11.12	14.3	17.32	16.7	18.65	16.3	6.20	55.8	16.8	1.33	7.7	-2.4	7.53	67.7	14.0
Managers	8.60	11.0	12.71	12.2	14.67	12.8	4.11	47.8	10.9	1.96	15.4	4.9	6.07	7.06	16.4
Sales workers	4.86	6.2	6.42	6.2	12.46	10.9	1.56	32.1	0.0	6.04	194.1	75.8	7.60	156.4	75.8
Clerical workers	13.18	16.9	18.22	17.5	17.77	15.5	5.04	38.2	3.6	-0.45	-2.5	-11.4	4.59	34.8	-8.3
Craft workers	10.43	13.4	13.10	12.6	13.40	11.7	2.67	25.6	-6.0	0.30	2.3	-7.1	2.97	28.5	-12.7
Operatives	10.20	13.1	11.07	10.7	8.37	7.3	0.87	8.6	-18.3	-2.70	-24.4	-31.8	-1.83	-17.9	-44.3
Transport workers	2.89	3.7	3.81	3.7	4.82	4.2	0.92	31.8	0.0	1.01	26.5	13.5	1.93	66.8	13.5
Laborers	3.58	4.6	4.30	4.1	4.45	3.9	0.72	20.1	-10.9	0.15	3.5	-4.9	0.87	24.3	-15.2
Service workers	8.62	11.1	12.30	11.8	13.08	11.4	3.68	42.7	6.3	0.78	6.3	-3.4	4.46	51.7	2.7
Other	3.37	4.3	2.85	2.7	3.77	3.3	-0.52	-15.4	-37.2	0.92	32.3	22.2	0.40	11.9	-23.3
Total	77.82		103.91		114.38		26.09	33.5		110.47	10.1		36.56	47.0	

Source and notes: Same as Table 4.1.

quarter of all jobs in 1970, fewer than a fifth by 1987. Indeed, the absolute number of manufacturing workers declined by almost a million between 1982 and 1987 alone (3.6 percent in relative terms). Two other sectors also lost significant shares of employment between 1970 and 1987, with the losses accelerating in the 1982–1987 period. Government employment expanded in tandem with the entire labor force between 1970 and 1982, but its share fell by 19 percent in the ensuing five years, no doubt reflecting the tenor of the Reagan presidency and its impact on state and local government as well. Likewise, the share of employment for agriculture, fisheries, and mining fell a scant 2.4 percent between 1970 and 1982, but then declined by more than 12 percent between 1982 and 1987 with the collapse of energy-related jobs.

While manufacturing (and later agriculture and government) employment was in retreat, jobs in services and the finance, real estate, and insurance sector boomed. The number of workers in services equaled the number in manufacturing in 1970, but by 1987 the number in services exceeded the number in manufacturing by more than twelve million, the former's share of all employment having increased by a fifth. Finance's gain in employment share was even greater, just shy of 30 percent from 1970 to 1987. The absolute number of workers in the finance, real estate, and insurance category almost doubled during this time.[9]

People migrate to jobs, literally in the sense that they will move long distances to find secure employment and figuratively in the sense that they will change occupations as technology changes. Such migration is nothing new: agricultural workers moved to urban areas as farming gave way to manufacture, and craft workers moved to new work sites as automation rendered their previous skills obsolete. However, the pace of change in the occupational distribution over the last two decades, reflecting the shift from manufacturing to services, was unprecedented (Table 4.2).[10]

[9]Since 1987, of course, growth in employment in both industries has abated, if not reversed, with the stock market crash and declining real estate values hitting finance and real estate employment first, and with absolute levels of service industry employment retreating during 1991 for the first time since the end of World War II (U.S. Department of Labor 1991a).

[10]Occupational codes are imprecise. The managerial category includes the 21-year-old night supervisor at a fast food restaurant and the CEO of a Fortune 500 company; service workers include the counter person at the fast food

In 1970, craft workers, operatives, and laborers comprised 31.1 percent of the labor force. After falling to 27.4 percent of all workers in 1982, by 1987 these manufacturing occupations constituted only 22.9 percent of all jobs, a loss of more than a quarter in their share of employment. Craft workers, as noted above, have suffered displacement for much of the last century, trends that continued at a relatively even pace in the two intervals 1970–1982 and 1982–1987. Likewise, automation has dislodged laborers for much of the post-World War II period. Operatives—the backbone of the modern factory and a highly paid one at that—have been hit hardest in recent years, however. Between 1982 and 1987 alone, the absolute number of machine operators fell by 24 percent, representing a loss of almost a third in their share of overall employment. Operatives experienced absolute losses of almost two million jobs and share losses of 44.3 percent between 1970 and 1987.

While craft workers, operatives, and laborers saw their share of employment decline, professionals, managers, and sales workers were on the rise, the former two occupations experiencing exceptional growth during the 1970–1982, the third during more recent years.[11] Between 1970 and 1982, the ranks of professionals expanded by more than six million and those of managers by more by four million, representing increases of more than 55 and 47 percent, respectively, in relative terms. Thus, even discounting code creep (calling some jobs "professional" or "managerial" dignifies them, the titles used to compensate for poor pay and working conditions), the transformation from manufacturing to services can hardly be said to have proletarianized the labor force.[12]

---

establishment and the celebrity chef at an exclusive restaurant. However, even accepting that coding is imprecise (and that coding conventions change), the magnitude of the shift from occupations prevalent in manufacturing to those prevalent in service industries is unmistakable.

[11]Again, coding conventions may account for part of the gain in employment share among professionals, managers, and sales workers, especially among the last. However, all data series show an increase of the same magnitude. For example, my analysis of the National Health Interview Survey indicated that sales workers experienced a 75.8 gain in their employment share for the period 1970 to 1987. The Current Population Survey data show the gain in share as 82.4 percent (U.S. Bureau of the Census 1972, 1984, 1990).

[12]Proletarianization of the labor force was predicted by Harry Braverman (1974) and by the sociologists Erik Wright and Jo Singleman (1982). However,

Indeed, the expansion of service occupations—those most emblematic of bad jobs—did not keep pace with the expansion of service industry employment. Service industry employment increased by three-quarters between 1970 and 1987, for a share gain of more than 18 percent. However, the share of employment represented by service occupations expanded by less than 3 percent (Table 4.2). More people may work for companies selling hamburgers (in reality business and health services grew faster), but many of these employees are shuffling paper, managing workers, or providing professional services, not selling french fries.

This situation may be changing, with the expansion of professional and managerial employment apparently coming to an end: between 1982 and 1987, the share of jobs accruing to professionals fell 2.4 percent, and the pace of increase among managers declined to half the 1970–1982 level. More contemporary employment data suggest that this trend continued beyond 1987, allowing the popular press to treat the current recession as an attack on middle management and professionals. In contrast to the pre-1987 years, the boom in employment in sales occupations also appears to have ended, no doubt reflecting the downturn in durable goods production and sales.[13]

One other trend in occupational employment bears noting. The strong demand for clerical and service occupations enabled millions of young women to enter the labor force. Between 1970 and 1982, absolute employment among clerical workers increased by more than five million, increasing this occupation's share of total employment by 3.6 percent. Service occupations expanded almost as much in absolute terms (and, given their smaller base, much more in relative terms) during this time. However, this "Great American Jobs Machine" is slowing down, signaling that the labor market may not be able to absorb many more new workers. The absolute number of clerical workers actually declined between 1982 and 1987, primarily because personal

Wright and Martin (1987) later wrote that the prediction had not materialized because the managerial and professional classifications had increased disproportionately, arguing that this change was inconsistent with the theory of proletarianization.

[13]See Haugen and Meisenheimer (1991) for the employment data. For an example of the articles in the general media about the effect of the recession on professionals and managers, see O'Boyle and Hymowitz 1990.

computers made clerical workers more productive, and service occupations expanded more slowly than did the labor force as a whole.

The quantitative shifts in employment among industries and occupations give no clue as to whether the mix of jobs included more "good" or "bad" ones at the end of the period under study than at the beginning. Manufacturing and construction certainly shed many good jobs, especially among operatives and crafts workers, but many of the new professional and managerial jobs in the finance, real estate, and insurance industries were also good ones. And while many of the new service jobs are no great shakes, many of the displaced laborers whose old jobs were either dirty or physically demanding would have gladly taken them even up in a trade had they been allowed to do so. However, without resolving the debate as to how the "jobs machine" affected the quality of work or the well-being of the overall economy, we do know that there has been a profound shift in what people do, with a steady erosion of manufacturing employment and later severe retrenchment in government, and with extraordinary growth in finance and other service-industry jobs. I now turn to the impact of this shift on those displaced from jobs they had held for a long time and on the terms of employment for all workers.

The Growth of the Rubber Band Labor Force

In the twenty-five years ending with the first energy crisis in 1973, productivity gains enabled the corporate sector to institute an implicit peace treaty with labor: workers could capture a fair share of increased earnings, in the form of both rising real wages (after compounding, wages rose about 50 percent a decade)[14] and increased pensions and benefits.[15] Most blue-collar workers experienced few periods of unemployment, and most stayed with the same firm, ceding control over work rules in exchange for senior-

[14]See Levy 1987, chapt. 4, especially 47–50.

[15]The expansion of private health insurance benefits, which was especially pronounced in the 1950s and 1960s, is described by Rosemary Stevens (1971, 426–432) and Paul Starr (1982, 290–339). William Graebner (1980) chronicles the development of the private pension system, and Stevens (1971) shows how government policy gave rise to the private pension and health insurance industries, principally through tax write-offs for these forms of compensation.

ity and higher wages. White-collar workers fared even better, not having to cede as much control over work to secure rising wages, and experiencing even fewer spells of unemployment. Thus, competitive success funded a bargain in which most workers stayed loyal to the firm (in the sense that they did not move among firms), most firms stayed loyal to the worker (in the sense that they resisted layoffs, and when they had to make them, they brought the worker back as soon as possible), and the bulk of employees enjoyed full-time, full-career jobs.

The energy crisis elicited a Pavlovian response from managers. By and large, corporations chose to jumpstart productivity by reducing the cost of the labor input rather than changing the mix of inputs. They used two basic strategies— albeit with many variants—to reduce labor costs: reduce the unit cost of labor by reducing wages and benefits; and make the units of labor used a variable, not constant, commodity, in effect tethering workers to the firm with a rubber band.[16]

The sudden drop in real hourly wages following the energy crisis—charted in the preceding chapter—attests to the short-term success of the first strategy; relatively stagnant wages in the years since, however, suggest that this did not jumpstart productivity. The U.S. record is especially poor given that other industrialized nations faced even higher energy prices, yet were able to achieve substantial productivity gains.[17] With hindsight, we can speculate that productivity lagged in the United States because management had asked workers to cede control over work for so long that when drawing upon workers' knowledge became one of the sources of productivity gain, neither workers nor management knew how to go about it.

Finding a way to get workers involved with production processes remains a daunting problem, especially given the strategy of severing the long-term commitment to employment in order to

[16]See Osterman 1988, especially chap. 3. Belous (1989) makes essentially the same point, albeit from a more contentious point of view.

[17]OECD data indicate that during the period 1973–1989, the non-U.S. members on average increased their manufacturing productivity, defined in terms of output per hour, by 19 percent more than did the U.S.; if the "sick nations" of Europe are eliminated from these calculations, the United States's successful competitors increased their average productivity by 29 percent more (U.S. Department of Labor 1991b).

make the labor input to production more responsive to market conditions. Management was even more successful in implementing this strategy than in implementing the wage-cutting one. The proportion of the labor force with full-time, full-career, full-benefit jobs with the same firm has been dramatically reduced. Conversely, more workers now face contingent employment. They will be brought in on a part-time or temporary basis when times are good, and quickly let go when the economy sours: thus, the rubber-band metaphor.

The modern employment lexicon reflects these changes.[18] Labor may be displaced (long-term workers let go, usually by the passive strategy of making temporary layoffs permanent or by outright plant closure), subcontracted (hired through an outside agency), contracted (hired through an employment-related subsidiary), leased (hired through an outside firm, and then leased to a firm on a semipermanent basis), pensioned off (at times through a golden handshake), hired as consultants (usually without benefits), and, in general, subjected to a reduction in force. Work may then be outsourced, even offshore, meaning that the work is to be done by another firm.[19] After implementing one or more of these strategies (which the casual observer might think involves turning nouns into verbs as much as reducing labor costs), the firm's labor force can be said to have been "downsized" or, more Orwellian yet, "rightsized." No firm uses all these strategies, but many use one or more of them, and most of the remaining ones threaten to use them even if they never actually do. Of course, part of the growth of contingent work reflects the ascendancy of service industries which have always used higher proportions of part-time and temporary workers. But part of the growth occurred among firms that formerly hired most workers on a permanent, full-time basis. Whatever the cause, contingent employment is on the rise.

[18]Belous (1989) is as much a dictionary of the terms used to connote the new set of labor arrangements as a description of them.

[19]Manufacturers have always purchased parts from suppliers, frequently being the supplier's only customer. However, now firms may call products their own when they played no part whatsoever in their manufacture. The car designed in Japan with parts made in Taiwan may get assembled in Mexico and still be sold by a U.S. company under its brand name. For a thorough description of this trend, see Osterman (1988, chap. 4).

Displaced Workers

The growth of service industries, as great as it has been, would not have been sufficient to account for the shift in the distribution of employment had manufacturing not shed workers. Thus, the plight of the displaced worker first came to prominence more than a decade ago when it became clear that large numbers of manufacturing workers were losing jobs, jobs they had held for a long time. Many of these workers were unable to find new jobs, and even among those able to find work, a plurality earned less than they had at their previous jobs.[20]

As a result of the publicity surrounding the problems of manufacturing workers, particularly those in the auto and steel industries, in 1984 the government began to collect data on the number of displaced workers, defined as those who left jobs held for more than three years.[21] Of course by that time, much of the damage had been done, the share of employment in manufacturing already having tumbled. Even so, the data on displaced workers are revealing both because they indicate that displacement has become the rule rather than the exception and because they demonstrate that the phenomenon is spreading to nonmanufacturing jobs.

The first survey of displaced workers covered the years 1979 through 1983, a period of intense recession and inflation; the second, the years 1983 through 1987, a period of economic expansion. Tables 4.3 and 4.4 summarize the results of the two surveys for industries and occupations, respectively. Not surprisingly, the displacement rate—the number of displaced workers divided by the number of all workers—fell by more than 15 percent with the end of the recession. Even so, more than 7 percent of the labor force, 4.629 million workers, suffered displacement in the years 1983 through 1987. The composition of the displacement changed

[20]Ibid., 21–24.

[21]The government collects data on displaced workers via a periodic supplement to the monthly *Current Population Survey*. See Flaim and Sehgal (1985); Horvath (1987); and Herz (1990) for reports on these surveys. Defining displaced workers as those losing jobs held for more than three years makes sense, insofar as workers with less tenure may not have chosen to remain in the same job for the remainder of their careers. However, many 20-year-old auto workers laid off in the 1970s would have been glad to make a career in the auto industry had that been an option. This being so, the government's definition of displacement underestimates the number of workers affected.

Table 4.3. Number and Rate of Displaced U.S. Workers by Industry, 1979–1983 and 1983–1987

Industry	1979–1983		1983–1987		Change	
	No. (millions)	Rate	No. (millions)	Rate	No. (millions)	Rate
Agricultural, fisheries, mining	0.150	20.2	0.215	31.7	.065	56.9
Construction	0.401	19.7	0.390	16.7	-.011	-15.2
Manufacturing	2.483	15.2	1.791	12.8	-.069	-15.8
Transportation, communications, utilities	0.336	9.2	0.292	7.5	-.044	-18.5
Wholesale/retail	0.732	8.7	0.930	10.0	.178	14.9
Finance, insurance, real estate	0.093	3.0	0.250	7.0	.157	133.3
Services	0.506	5.6	0.574	5.3		-5.4
Farming	0.100	12.4	0.046	5.4	-.054	-56.5
Government	0.248	2.2	0.136	1.2	-.112	-45.5
Total	5.091	8.5	4.629	7.2	-.462	-15.3

Source: Author's reanalysis of data from Herz 1990.
Note: The displacement rate is the proportion of all displaced workers in an industry or occupation divided by that industry's or occupation's proportion of all workers.

Table 4.4. Number and Rate of Displaced U.S. Workers by Occupation, 1979–1983 and 1983–1987

Occupation	1979–1983		1983–1987		Change	
	No. (millions)	Rate	No. (millions)	Rate	No. (millions)	Rate
Professionals	0.260	3.1	0.292	3.1	.032	0.0
Managers	0.444	6.0	0.524	6.1	.080	01.7
Technical workers	0.122	6.9	0.165	8.4	.043	21.7
Sales workers	0.468	8.0	0.508	7.5	.040	–06.3
Clerical workers	0.572	6.0	0.645	6.5	.073	08.3
Service workers	0.275	4.5	0.312	4.8	.037	06.7
Craft workers	1.042	12.9	0.833	9.6	–.209	–25.6
Operatives	1.144	21.1	0.751	14.9	–.393	–29.4
Transport workers	0.324	12.0	0.323	11.7	–.001	–02.5
Laborers	0.355	17.4	0.227	11.3	–.128	–35.1
Farm workers	0.058	2.7	0.050	2.0	–.018	–25.9
Total	5.091	8.5	4.629	7.2	–.462	–15.3

Source and note: Same as Table 4.3.

as well. In the first period under study, more than 60 percent of displaced workers had been in the agricultural, mining, construction, and manufacturing industries. The proportion of all displaced workers in these industries declined to 50 percent during the second. Although displacement rates remained higher in these industries, wholesale/retail and finance, insurance, and real estate registered the largest gains, suggesting that displacement had become a more generalized strategy as the years unfolded. Recall from Table 4.1 that wholesale/retail employment increased by almost two million over the same time period, and then note that almost a million workers were displaced from this industry in those years of rapid expansion. Losing jobs held a long time when industries decline is one thing; losing them when expansion occurs is unprecedented.

Displacement spread among occupations, too. In the 1979 to 1983 period, craft workers, operatives, and laborers comprised 56 percent of all displaced workers; by the second period, their share had fallen to 46 percent, 20 percent less in relative terms. All the occupations with greater numbers of displaced workers in the second period were white-collar ones; all with fewer displaced workers were blue-collar classifications. Again, displacement rates were not necessarily tied to decline in employment. Between 1982 and 1987, the number of managers rose by more than two million, an increase of about 5 percent in this occupation's share of all employment, but more than half a million managers were displaced during these years.

These data from the government surveys suggest that in the early period displacement was tied more closely to economic decline, but in the second period, displacement became a mechanism to reallocate workers among industries, occupations, and firms, some of which were ascending. Whether or not this is true, by the second period under study, displacement had spread from goods- to service-producing environments, belying the notion that only manufacturing workers experienced this phenomenon.

The Growth of Contingent Work Arrangements

Labor market analysts differ in their definitions of contingency, and, hence, in their estimates of its magnitude and spread. Belous (1989) defines contingent work by exclusion: all those self-employed and all in jobs that are not permanent, full-time positions work contingently.[22] Polivka and Nardone (1989) argue that many jobs subsumed within Belous's definition are not contingent, merely something other than full-time salary or wage positions. They define contingent workers as those with little job security, and hence those lacking a long-term commitment from an employer. However, their definition may be too exclusive, since few contracts explicitly cover the security of employment (and many that do cover it, such as those in the auto, steel, rail, and printing trades are under attack). Osterman (1988) takes a more functional approach: workers with more benefits, security, and permanence form a "core" of employees, while those with less are in "peripheral" positions (he does not define the quantities necessary to pass this screen, however.).[23]

These disagreements do not matter: what matters is that increasing proportions of the labor force do not know where they will be working tomorrow, what the length of their work week will be, or what mix of pay and benefits they can expect. Furthermore, many had this kind of certainty when their careers began, or so they thought. Whether or not their current work meets strict criteria for contingency, their expectations are contingent in so far as they and their current employers lack commitment to each other.

Contingent work takes many forms, some easy to define and quantify from labor market data (for example, the extent of involuntary part-time work and unemployment and the proportion of jobs providing pension and health insurance coverage), some difficult to define but relatively easy to measure once defined (for example, the proportion of employees not directly hired by firms), some both difficult to define and difficult to measure (for example, the spread of uncertainty about future employment). I will concentrate on the first category, since my point is not to define or

[22]Belous (1989) enumerated between 29 million and 37 million contingent workers in 1988, most of whom were self-employed and/or in part-time jobs. However, he argues that the fastest growing segments of the contingent labor force are temporary and contract employees.

[23]Polivka and Nardone (1989) note that this definition is remarkably similar to the Marxian notion of a dual labor market, in which one set of workers is accorded privileged (and protected) status and the others are allocated to lower-paying jobs with little security and few benefits. Cain (1976) provides a thorough review of this literature.

exactly quantify contingent arrangements, but to show that the uncertainty associated with contingency is spreading.[24]

It is true that many workers consider the uncertainty an acceptable trade-off for the flexibility that accompanies much contingent work. Temporary or part-time positions allow someone to accommodate child or elder care responsibilities[25] and many workers will forgo benefits at their jobs since their spouses have good pension and health insurance coverage. Nevertheless, the

---

[24]Belous (1989, 15–17) argues that the expansion of the temporary help and business services industries is evidence that firms contract for services their own employees once performed. He notes that employment in the temporary help industry expanded by 175 percent between 1980 and 1988, to 1.1 million workers; in the business services, it increased by 70 percent, to 5.6 million. See also Carey and Hazelbaker (1986), for estimates of the growth in the temporary help industry. Osterman (1988) agrees that the expansion of temporary help and business services follow firms' desire to reduce the number of workers to whom they have long-term and permanent commitments. Polivka and Nardone (1989), however, see the growth of business services more as an expression of economies of scale in such functions as payroll, data processing, security, and janitorial service than as a desire to externalize labor costs (though they do not deny that the latter plays a part). They also make the point that many business services firms provide secure employment with good benefits, so that what is contingent from the perspective of the firm contracting for these services may not be from the perspective of the person who works for a business services company. Indeed, were a small firm to hire someone to do payroll, that person would likely only work part-time. Thus, the growth of business services could reflect a less contingent labor force. Some analysts cite the growth in self-employment as another example of the spread of contingency, insofar as it is assumed that individual entrepreneurs cannot buffer the economic environment as well as the big firm can (nor can they pay as much or provide as many benefits). Nonagricultural self-employment has risen sharply in the last two decades, from a low of 6.1 percent of the labor force in the early 1970s to 7.0 percent in 1988, an increase of 15 percent (U.S. Bureau of the Census, 1990, 380, 382, 387). Analysts differ as to the implications of this increase, some holding that most of the new self-employed are tethered to large firms in contractual arrangements, more evidence for the growth of contingency (Linder and Houghton 1990), others arguing that the growth occurred disproportionately in "post-industrial" sectors and, as such, is an outgrowth of the kinds of industries that are expanding rather than a part of employment policy per se (Steinmetz and Wright 1989).

[25]See, for example, Blank (1990, 123) for the argument that women may choose part-time work because it allows "flexible work hours, additional income, and continued labor market involvement while still permitting pursuit of significant activities outside the labor market." See also Shank 1986.

growth in the involuntary component of contingency outstripped the growth of the voluntary, suggesting that most workers took contingent positions because that is all they were offered. I will begin with the evidence concerning part-time employment (Table 4.5), since the growth of part-time work is central to the argument that contingency is growing. In the early 1970s, the part-time share of employment averaged 13.4 percent of the labor force, and about a fifth of part-time employment was involuntary (labeled "due to economic reasons" in the Census Bureau surveys). In the five years ending in 1987, part-timers comprised 16.0 percent of the labor force, and just under 40 percent of them were in this position involuntarily. This was not a cyclical phenomenon, since both periods were expansionary. Indeed, the part-time component of the labor force in the years surrounding the 1981 recession only exceeded that in the expansionary period by 2 percent, and the fraction attributable to involuntary part-time employment was actually lower. The growth of all forms of part-time employment was especially pronounced among men (37 percent between the early 1970s and pre-1987 period), with the involuntary component increasing from a third to a half. The proportion of all women in part-time employment remained constant between the two periods, but the involuntary component expanded from less than 16 percent of all part-time workers in the early 1970s to more than a quarter in the five years preceding 1987.

The evidence concerning the nature of unemployment tells much the same story (Table 4.6). In the second expansionary period as compared to the first, the overall unemployment rate rose a little, but the proportion of unemployment due to a lost job soared, averaging slightly more than 40 percent in the early 1970s, but more than 50 percent in the five years before 1987. The involuntary component increased for both men and women, about 20 percent in both cases. The duration of unemployment also lengthened as the years passed, and the lengthening continued even with the economic expansion in the mid- and late 1980s. Spells of unemployment typically lasted ten weeks in the early 1970s; in the years surrounding the recession of 1981, they lasted fourteen; in the five years preceding 1987, they averaged more than sixteen weeks.

Thus, part-time work expanded (at least among men), and more of it was involuntary. At the same time, spells of unemployment

Table 4.5. Proportion of the U.S. Labor Force with Part-time Work by Sex and Reason, 1970–1987

Year	All workers			Men			Women		
	%	Due to econ-%	Usual FT-%	%	Due to econ-%	Usual FT-%	%	Due to econ-%	Usual FT-%
1970	13.2	2.8	1.7	6.3	2.2	1.6	24.6	3.7	1.8
1971	13.5	3.1	1.6	6.5	2.4	1.5	25.0	4.2	1.8
1972	13.3	2.8	1.4	6.4	2.1	1.3	24.7	3.9	1.6
1973	13.3	2.7	1.3	6.3	2.0	1.2	24.6	3.7	1.5
1974	13.8	3.1	1.7	6.7	2.4	1.6	25.0	4.2	1.8
1975	15.0	4.1	2.1	7.8	3.4	2.1	25.9	5.2	2.1
1976	14.5	3.6	1.6	7.3	2.9	1.6	25.3	4.7	1.6
1977	14.5	3.5	1.5	7.3	2.7	1.5	25.1	4.7	1.5
1978	14.2	3.3	1.4	6.9	2.4	1.4	24.7	4.5	1.5
1979	14.2	3.4	1.4	6.9	2.5	1.4	24.5	4.6	1.5
1980	15.1	4.1	1.9	8.0	3.3	1.9	24.8	5.1	1.8
1981	16.3	4.5	1.9	8.1	3.6	2.0	25.3	5.6	1.8
1982	17.1	6.0	2.3	9.7	5.0	2.6	26.8	7.2	2.1
1983	16.8	5.9	2.0	9.6	4.8	2.1	26.4	7.4	1.8
1984	16.0	5.3	1.7	8.8	4.2	1.8	25.2	6.6	1.6
1985	15.8	5.0	1.7	8.6	3.9	1.7	25.0	6.3	1.6
1986	16.0	4.9	1.6	8.7	3.9	1.7	25.0	6.1	1.5
1987	15.5	4.6	1.5	8.5	3.7	1.6	24.1	5.7	1.4

Source: Author's analysis of data from U.S Department of Labor 1985b, 6–7; id. 1988b, 710–712; U.S. Bureau of the Census 1990, 380.
Notes: % = percent working part-time; due to econ. = working part-time for economic reasons; usual Ft = working part-time, but usually work full-time.

Table 4.6. Unemployment in the U.S. Labor Force: Number, Rate, Reason, and Average Duration by Sex, 1970–1987

	Total				Men			Women		
	Unemployed		Of unemployed…		Unemployed		Of unemployed…	Unemployed		Of unemployed…
Year	No.	%	% Who lost job	Duration	No.	%	% Who lost job	No.	%	% Who lost job
1970	4.088	4.8	44.3	8.8	2.235	4.2	53.6	1.853	5.9	33.1
1971	4.994	5.8	41.9	11.4	2.776	5.1	50.1	2.217	6.9	31.6
1972	4.840	5.5	43.2	12.1	2.635	4.8	52.2	2.205	6.6	32.3
1973	4.304	4.7	38.7	10.0	2.240	4.0	48.2	2.064	5.9	28.3
1974	5.076	5.4	43.4	9.7	2.668	4.7	53.8	2.408	6.6	32.0
1975	7.830	8.2	55.4	14.2	4.385	7.6	65.6	3.445	9.2	42.5
1976	7.288	7.5	49.7	15.8	3.968	6.8	60.2	3.320	8.5	37.2
1977	6.855	6.8	45.3	14.3	3.588	6.0	55.1	3.267	8.0	34.5
1978	6.047	5.8	41.6	11.9	3.051	5.0	51.5	2.996	7.0	31.4
1979	5.963	5.6	42.9	11.9	3.018	4.9	53.4	2.945	6.6	32.1
1980	7.448	6.9	51.8	11.9	4.157	6.6	62.3	3.291	7.2	38.6
1981	8.273	7.5	51.6	13.7	4.577	7.2	61.6	3.696	7.9	39.1
1982	10.678	9.5	58.7	15.6	6.179	9.7	69.2	4.499	9.4	44.2
1983	10.717	9.5	58.4	20.0	6.260	9.7	69.2	4.457	9.2	43.2
1984	8.538	7.5	51.8	18.2	4.744	7.4	62.7	3.794	7.6	38.1
1985	8.312	7.2	49.8	15.6	4.521	7.0	60.8	3.791	7.4	36.7
1986	8.237	7.0	49.0	15.0	4.530	6.9	60.2	3.707	7.1	35.3
1987	7.425	6.1	48.0	14.5	4.101	6.2	59.3	3.324	6.0	34.1

Source: Author's analysis of data from U.S Bureau of the Census 1975, 349, 351; id. 1981, 391; id. 1988, 383; id. 1989a, 393–394; U.S. Department of Labor 1988b, 723.

Notes: No. = number of unemployed in millions; % = percent of labor force unemployed; lost job = involuntary loss of employment; % of unemployed = % of unemployed who lost jobs involuntarily; duration = average duration of unemployment in months.

Table 4.7. U.S. Workers Covered by Employer-Provided Pensions and
Group Health Insurance, 1980–1987

	Pensions		Group health insurance	
Year	No. (millions)	%	No. (millions)	%
1980	48.003	44.9	66.291	61.9
1981	47.679	44.3	66.778	62.0
1982	46.799	43.8	65.942	61.7
1983	47.080	43.4	66.167	61.0
1984	47.490	42.4	66.964	59.8
1985	48.959	42.8	68.914	60.2
1986	49.578	42.6	70.000	60.1
1987	48.195	40.8	66.822	56.6

Source: Author's analysis of data from U.S. Bureau of the Census 1983b, 406; id. 1984, 436; id. 1985, 421; id. 1986, 421; id. 1987, 405; id. 1988, 396; id. 1989, 409; id. 1990, 413.

lengthened, with more of them the result of job loss rather than a temporary layoff or the desire to switch jobs. Contingent work arrangements may offer flexibility, but this involuntary flexibility is not what most workers had in mind.

Nor is it likely that millions of workers freely chose to forgo the protection of pension and health insurance coverage, especially in a time of rising health care costs and economic uncertainty. The growth of these benefits, hailed as a triumph of the private sector approach to social security, had been the hallmark of post–World War II employment.[26] The proportion of the labor force covered by pensions and health insurance, however, reached its zenith in the early 1980s, with about 45 percent receiving the former and 62 percent the latter at that time (Table 4.7). In part reflecting the growth of part-time employment, in part the growth of service sector jobs, in part the growth of self-employment, and in part the rising cost of pensions and health care, the fraction of the labor force with retirement and health benefits fell by about 10 percent in the 1980s. The loss of health benefits has been well chronicled in the press because the uninsured population can only delay medical treatment for so long before they make demands on the public hospital system, a process that has already run its course;

[26]See Stevens 1988.

Table 4.8. Union Membership of the U.S. Labor Force, 1970–1987

Year	Union members	
	No.	**%**
1970	19.381	27.3
1972	19.435	26.4
1974	20.199	25.8
1976	19.634	24.5
1978	20.246	23.6
1980	20.968	23.2
1981	–	–
1982	19.571	21.9
1983	17.717	20.1
1984	17.340	18.8
1985	16.996	18.0
1986	16.975	17.5
1987	16.193	17.2

Source: Author's analysis of data from U.S. Bureau of the Census 1983b, 409; id. 1984, 439; id. 1987, 409; id. 1988, 401–402; id. 1989, 415–416.
Note: Dash indicates data not available.

the loss of pension coverage, a stealth problem if there ever was one, will be noted only as young workers newly hired in the 1980s begin to retire several decades from now.

The decline in the proportion of the labor force covered by pensions and health insurance, sharp as it is, pales in comparison to the decline in union membership. The fraction of the labor force enrolled in unions peaked in 1970, before declining by more than 37 percent in the interim. The absolute number of union members hit an all-time high of about 21 million in 1980, before falling by 4.75 million workers, or 23 percent, in the ensuing years (Table 4.8). Whatever one thinks of unions, they do negotiate standardized wages and conditions, frequently for entire industries, thus reducing the variance in compensation.[27] Moreover, unions have always sought to have employers make layoffs on the basis of seniority. Under the system they negotiated, workers with the longest job tenure retain full-time jobs, and those with the

[27]See Osterman (1988, especially 41–44).

least tenure are laid off entirely. The growth in part-time employment and other contingent arrangements may reflect the erosion in the unionized share of the labor force.

Pulling Apart

As a result of the changes in the labor market, more people work, but fewer have full-time, full-benefit jobs, fewer escape long spells of unemployment, fewer feel secure that they will have well-remunerated work tomorrow, and fewer can anticipate having a pension on which to retire. Neither the gain in labor force participation rates nor the loss of secure, well-remunerated employment was an equal opportunity phenomenon. The result has been a growing inequality of both income and earnings—what some have called the "pulling apart" of society. In this section, I describe the distributional aspects of labor market dynamics, emphasizing the groups systematically bypassed by the expansion of labor force participation rates, and those who work, but for a declining share of earnings.

Discussion of income and earnings distributions, formerly relegated to academia, has gone public. Frank Levy (1987) attributes this newfound interest in issues of equality to a profound sense of malaise brought about by the slow growth in incomes in the years after the first oil shock in 1973.[28] The form this interest takes, however, has changed. In the early 1980s, the prevailing wisdom was that we had taxed away the incentive for rich people to save and invest, to do well for all of us by doing well for themselves, a view turned into policy with the election of Ronald Reagan.[29] David Stockman later called the strategy a Trojan horse, an excuse to transfer money to the wealthy without much thought as to the costs and benefits of doing so. When the tide carrying the rich failed to raise all boats, attention shifted from the plight of those at the top of the income distribution to those at the bottom. Some looked at the income dynamics and saw the opportunity for political gain in attacking the wealthy,[30] but most analysts were gen-

[28]See Levy 1987, chap. 1, especially 1–5.

[29]The two principal proponents of this view were George Gilder (1981) in his *Wealth and Poverty,* and Charles Murray (1984) in his *Losing Ground.*

[30]The point of Kevin Phillips's (1990) popular book, *The Politics of Rich and Poor,* is that class politics will redound to the Democrats in the years to

uinely concerned with the plight of those whose share of income had declined, frequently to a point below the poverty line.[31]

The growing inequality of incomes is fact, easily proven with whatever measure chosen. The reasons for the growing inequality are many, each debatable and each debated. Some claim that the inequality derives from extraordinary growth among the wealthy, but not at the expense of the middle class or the poor.[32] Others see polarization, with more of the middle class reaching affluence and more falling to near the poverty line.[33] Still others are convinced that the bottom has dropped out, citing not only income statistics but the obvious pathology of the urban ghetto and the emergence of homelessness and childhood hunger and illness to make their case. The sociologist William Julius Wilson (1987) may be the best known proponent of this view.[34] Wilson argues that the loss of manufacturing jobs destabilized poor (especially black) communities, robbing them of the working-class fraction that

---

come, just as racial politics redounded to the Republicans in the last two decades.

[31]David Ellwood (1988) argues for policies designed to make work pay by supplementing low wages enough to bring earnings above the poverty level, thus echoing Daniel Moynihan's controversial proposals from the 1960s (see Moynihan, 1973) which were recently given new life by William Julius Wilson's (1987) *The Truly Disadvantaged.*

[32]See Rosenthal (1985) for the argument that the proportion of good-paying jobs has increased; Juhn et al. (cited in Ryscavage and Henle 1990) argue that this was the result of increasing returns to education.

[33]See, for example, Blackburn, Bloom, and Freeman (1990, 1991), Burtless (1987), and Levy (1987) for the data indicating that those at the bottom of the income distribution saw their share erode, while those at the top of the distribution increased their share of income.

[34]In this view, a fraction of the population has become so isolated that they have few connections to the norms of "middle-class" behavior and constitute an "underclass" of increasing proportions. As used in the lay press, the term *underclass* connotes many things: for some, a set of individuals so beyond the pale that we can do little but lock them up or isolate them; for others, a set of perfect victims; for still others, a group condemned to immobility by a culture of poverty rather than by a lack of opportunity. Wilson (1987, especially chap. 1) presents each of the arguments about the scope of the "underclass" and the cause of their plight. Mincy, Sawhill, and Wolf (1990) recently reviewed academic estimates of the size of the "underclass," including those isolated by persistent or concentrated poverty, in either case accompanied by dysfunctional behavior. They found that by any definition the "underclass" is a small fraction of the entire population, let alone of the poor, but that it is growing.

brought values, institutions, and, yes, money to their neighbor-
hoods.[35] The declining value of transfer payments accelerated
this process in recent years, making life harder, but the train had
begun going downhill long before this, since the erosion of the
manufacturing sector preceded the concerted attack on the welfare state by many years.

Haveman and Wolfe (1989) make a similar argument with respect to disability. During the 1960s and early 1970s, the demand
for labor grew, pulling more of the disabled into the labor market,
and raising their earnings. In the years that followed, the labor
force participation of the disabled fell, but relatively high
disability transfer payments replaced some of the lost earnings. In
the 1980s, however, the cushion of transfer payments was removed, dramatically worsening the income of the disabled, leaving them with much lower incomes relative to the population
without disabilities than in either of the two previous periods.

In the Wilson and Haveman-Wolfe scenarios, the bottom fell out
for ghetto residents and people with disabilities when the jobs
moved away (literally in the case of the former, figuratively in the
case of the latter). One could paint a similar picture for many
other groups systematically left out of the jobs picture, including
minority youth wherever they may live, older workers displaced
from long-held jobs, particularly in the industrial belt, and, more
recently, those who were part of the services and high tech boom
during the early and mid-1980s.[36]

But the effect of changes in employment patterns on incomes
was not limited to those who lost their jobs altogether. Also
affected were many working people, indeed, many who were
working full-time.[37] Between the early 1970s and the late 1980s,
the proportion of workers earning a "living wage" (defined by the
official poverty line) fell substantially. This could have happened
simply because the earnings of all workers stagnated after 1973,

---

[35]The notion that ghettos are at a remove from employment opportunities is
also called the spatial mismatch thesis. Much of the evidence to support the
spatial mismatch hypothesis comes from the work of John Kasarda (1989,
1990); some counterevidence derives from Ellwood (1986).

[36]See Tables 4.3 and 4.4 for estimates of the number of workers displaced
from the growth industries of the early and mid-1980s. For a description of
their plight, see Swaim and Podgursky (1989).

[37]Levy 1987, 99-100; and Ellwood 1986, chapt. 4.

forcing those at the bottom of the distribution to fall below the cutoff for a poverty income. It could have, but it didn't. Instead, workers in the bottom quintile of the earnings distribution got a smaller slice of the pie. For example, the share of aggregate earnings accruing to the bottom quintile of full-time workers fell 12 percent among men and 17 percent among women between 1978 and 1988 (Ryscavage and Henle 1990). Although one can pick a set of figures that paints a somewhat rosier picture, the weight of the evidence supports the view that earnings—like income—grew more unequal after 1980.[38]

[38]Ryscavage and Henle (1990) review the literature and update their own earlier analysis (see Henle and Ryscavage 1980), concluding that earnings were distributed more unevenly at the close of the decade. In their own analysis, they calculate the change in the earnings distribution three ways: by estimating the share of earnings accruing to each quintile in different years, by estimating the percentage change in earnings for each quintile, and by calculating the Gini index for all workers and for full-time workers. The Gini index, which ranges from 0, perfect equality, to 1, all income accruing to one person, is the most widely used measure of inequality. The Gini index for all workers rose slightly between 1978 and 1988, from .468 to .469 (the rise among men was much more severe, from .413 to .441, and the rise among women was also substantial, from .446 to .451). Inequality increased much more among full-time workers than among all workers, from .312 in 1978 to .343 in 1988 (the increase among full-time men was from .296 to .337, and that for full-time women was from .240 to .296). Thus, analysts wishing to pooh-pooh the notion that earnings are growing more unequal will cite the Gini index for all workers, rather than evaluating the change in share accruing to each quintile of all workers and full-time workers, or rather than citing the Gini index for full-time workers. Ryscavage and Henle (1990) conclude that the latter statistic is the most telling, since it measures the predicament of those with the most attachment to the labor force and, generally, the greatest family responsibilities. See also Blackburn, Bloom, and Freeman 1991.

The reasons for the growing inequality of earnings are not so clear. At least four explanations have been argued: the size of the baby boom cohort is driving down the wages at the bottom of the pay scale (Levy 1987; Lawrence 1985); the proportion of lower-paying jobs is declining (Rosenthal 1985); the proportion of lower-paying jobs is rising partly because of shifts from manufacturing to services and the greater variance in incomes within the services sector (Harrison and Bluestone 1988); and in an apparent resolution of the last two theses, the proportion of lower-paying jobs is increasing within each occupation and industry, even though the economy may be shifting to higher-paying industries and occupations, with the former process outstripping the latter (McMahon and Tschetter 1986). One thing that is clear is that the economy rewards the skilled relative to the unskilled much more handsomely

Some view the growing dispersion of wages as the inevitable outcome of the shift to services. The service sector harbors both the disabled boy working for McDonald's in their now famous commercial and the Harvard Business School professor advising Fortune 500 companies on investment strategy. Others attribute growing inequality to the declining share of workers protected by union contracts, a change that may or may not be the inevitable result of the shift away from manufacturing. Unions negotiate standardized contracts in which job tenure alone affects wages. More firms now use merit-based pay, resulting in greater variance within levels of tenure.

Several factors are no doubt at play since the variance in earnings between industries and even within occupations has increased dramatically in the last two decades. Tables 4.9 and 4.10 chart the industry and occupation data, respectively. In 1970, the industry with the lowest wages for full-time workers (retail trade) paid about 42 percent as much as the industry with the highest wages (utilities). This ratio subsequently fell, to 39 percent in 1982, and to 34 percent in 1987. Thus, more of us work in poor-paying sectors, and the poor-paying sectors pay even more poorly than they used to. If all else had been equal, the extensive growth of retail and service employment ought to have bid up wages in these sectors relative to other industries. All else was not equal, however, since wages in services grew very little and wages in retail fell substantially.

Starting in 1990, firms could pay workers under age 16 starting their first jobs less than the standard minimum wage. The passage of this legislation merely extended to those at the absolute bottom of the earnings distribution the now widespread practice of paying new hires less. To a certain extent, new hires have always been paid less, but the ratio of their earnings relative to those already on the job has been falling. White-collar workers are not immune to the trend. Thus, for all but one of the white-collar occupations for which federal data are available, entry-level workers make less relative to those in more senior classifications than they did two decades age. Some of the changes are stunning. Senior-level ac-

---

than in the past, and that this effect remains strong whether one measures skill in terms of education or occupation (Blackburn, Bloom, and Freeman 1990).

Table 4.9. Average U.S. Wages and Salaries per Full-time-Equivalent Employee by Industry, 1970, 1982, and 1987 (1987 dollars)

Industry	1970	1982	1987
Agriculture	12,359	12,978	11,877
Mining	27,674	33,651	33,922
Construction	28,743	25,765	24,586
Manufacturing	24,553	24,869	26,356
Transportation	27,551	27,652	26,377
Communications	25,640	30,686	34,463
Electric, gas, sanitation, utilities	29,365	31,383	34,786
Wholesale	26,936	25,628	27,275
Retail	17,328	14,574	14,586
Finance, insurance, real estate	22,916	22,327	27,612
Services	18,734	19,123	21,013
Government	23,472	22,311	23,993
Ratio of lowest/highest	.42	.39	.34

Source: Author's analysis of data from U.S. Bureau of the Census 1984, 431; id. 1990, 406, 470.

Table 4.10. Ratio of Wages between Highest and Lowest Classifications of U.S. Occupations, 1970, 1982, and 1988

Occupation	1970	1982	1988
Accountants	1.82	2.12	3.08
Attorneys	2.78	3.02	3.23
Buyers	1.63	1.84	1.96
Job analysts	1.46	1.68	1.61
Directors of personnel	1.74	1.85	2.08
Chemists	2.50	2.73	2.99
Engineers	2.48	2.64	2.98

Source: Author's analysis of data from U.S. Department of Labor 1985b, 324–327; id. 1988c, 39–41.

Table 4.11. Educational Attainment of the U.S. Labor Force by Sex, 1970, 1982, and 1987 (percentage distribution)

Group	1970	1982	1987
All workers			
Less than high school	36	22	15
High school	38	41	40
Some college	12	18	20
College	14	19	25
Men			
Less than high school	38	23	17
High school	35	38	37
Some college	12	17	19
College	16	21	27
Women			
Less than high school	34	19	13
High school	44	45	44
Some college	11	19	21
College	11	17	23

Source: Author's analysis of data from U.S. Bureau of the Census 1984, 411; id. 1990, 379.

Note: Percentages do not total 100 because of rounding.

countants' advantage over those beginning their careers grew by 70 percent between 1970 and 1988, and it was not puny to begin with; senior attorneys, scientists, and engineers also experienced tremendous growth in earnings at the expense of their junior colleagues.

At the same time that employers paid new workers less, they required them to go to school longer. Of course, the demand for workers with less than a high school education slackened the most, in the process bidding down their wages disproportionately to the remainder of the labor force and contributing to the loss of income share among those at the bottom of the earnings distribution. Between 1970 and 1987, the proportion of all labor force participants with less than twelve years of schooling declined from 36 to 15 percent (Table 4.11). In contrast, the proportion who had attended college almost doubled (it more than doubled among women). Thus, it took much more schooling to get a job, even though going to college became more expensive as the years went by. However, there were no alternatives, since employers were able to demand college attendance for occupations that formerly did not require that level of education (Table 4.12). For example, the proportion of clerical and sales workers with a college degree more than doubled between 1970 and 1987. Employers were even able to demand more schooling of the least skilled. The proportion of operatives and laborers with less than a high school education fell by about half (similar declines occurred among craft, service, and farm workers). Ironically, employers demanded more schooling, but complained that their new workers were inadequately trained in the most basic skills. The cost of education grew, but the outcome of education cheapened.

Summary

Bell (1973) and Gartner and Riessman (1974) began a debate two decades ago about the meaning of the shift to services, Bell arguing that it could mean that brain power and social organization would become the engine for economic development, Gartner and Riessman warning that most services had nothing to do with economic development. Many have joined the debate in the interim, but no one has resolved it. There are many trends for both sides to latch onto, and much that appears contradictory. Older workers have suffered displacement, but the premium paid to senior workers has grown. The labor force participation rate has expanded, incorporating millions of new entrants, particularly women, but several groups have been systematically bypassed in the process, including nonwhite men and manufacturing workers, and the fraction employed part-time involuntarily has grown. Manufacturing and manufacturing occupations contracted, and services and service occupations expanded. However, even the services boom seems fraught with contradictions, growth having occurred in the business services sector (presumably a good trend) and in the fast food, security, and building services industries (presumably a bad one). We have been warned that bad jobs are proliferating while witnessing the expansion of the managerial and professional ranks and heightened educational requirements. Finally, we have been told both that the sum of the changes has left the labor force at the mercy of the economic winds, a just-in-time inventory of people as well as parts, and that we have marginalized (and alienated) increasing fractions of the labor

Table 4.12. Educational Attainment of the U.S. Labor Force by Occupation and Sex, 1970, 1982, and 1987

	Men						Women					
	Less than high school			College or more			Less than high school			College or more		
Occupation	1970	1982	1987	1970	1982	1987	1970	1982	1987	1970	1982	1987
Professionals and managers	15	5	3	43	57	66	12	4	2	45	51	57
Clerical and sales workers	27	10	7	14	28	31	23	9	6	4	10	14
Craft workers	52	26	23	2	6	6	53	21	23	1	6	3
Operatives and laborers	65	40	32	1	1	4	69	49	37	1	5	5
Service workers	59	30	23	3	10	11	63	40	30	2	7	7
Farm workers	65	43	38	3	11	8				65	23	31

Source: Author's analysis of data from U.S. Bureau of the Census 1972, 230; id. 1984, 418–420; id. 1988, 378.

Note: Percentages do not total 100 because of omitted categories.

force, eroding workers' commitment to their firms. It is possible, of course, to see all these contradictions as a set of jumbled wires, the emergence of the post-industrial society requiring us to put disparate trends together in different combinations.[39]

We will probably never resolve the debate about what the trends in the labor market portend for the future, let alone whether they are good for the economy now. But we do know they have rendered work life fundamentally different. A few decades ago, most workers were involved with goods production, stayed with their firms for most of their careers (and expected to do so), received the same pay as the bulk of the other workers in their firm or industry, had full-time jobs and full health and pension benefits, experienced few and short spells of unemployment, and most important, felt secure in all of this. The sense of security is gone. Many workers experienced the objective changes that eroded their security, and even those who did not experience them worry about them. Having described this loss of security, I now turn to its implications for the day-to-day conduct of work.

[39]This is the argument first made by Larry Hirschhorn (1975) in the mid-1970s and then reiterated by Fred Block (1990). In between, Hirschhorn (1984, 1988) and Zuboff (1988) described the environment at the level of the firm and the society necessary to unlock the developmental potential of the service economy.

5

Industrial Working Conditions in a Post-Industrial Age

Present-day work mirrors the U.S. factory environment during the twentieth century, both because the factory was numerically dominant as the situs of employment and because the nonindustrial sectors of the economy are adopting the factory system of management-employee relations.[1] I argue that we have transposed

---

[1]This chapter, unlike all the others, argues without reference to statistical information, drawing a picture of qualitative changes in work from a reading of the literature, by making inferences from the quantitative information presented in Chapter 4, and from discussions with labor market experts. I have purposefully overemphasized factory work in this description, in the belief that the factory looms larger in determining working conditions in the remainder of economy than the sheer numbers of manufacturing workers would indicate. However, the factory has never been completely dominant as a situs of employment and has receded in importance with the erosion of manufacturing. Nevertheless, the other sectors do take their cues from factory working conditions, the insurance industry claims office, the welfare bureaucracy, and the fast food outlet being some prominent examples of this. Moreover, the argument overstylizes the two eras of factory work described, in effect denying the considerable autonomy left to workers on the assembly line as well as the majority of workers who were never actually on the line in the Taylor/Ford factory system, while overemphasizing the freedom given workers in the new factory organized on the principles of continuous improvement. In describing the factory during different eras, I have relied upon several classic works, including the descriptions of the original Hawthorne studies by George Homans's (1950) *The Human Group,* Chris Argyris's (1982) *Reasoning, Learning, and Action: Individual and Organizational,* and David Noble's (1986) *Forces of Production: A Social History of Industrial Automation,* all of which take a human relations approach to the workplace, and

the working conditions traditionally associated with manufacturing to the other sectors of the economy when we should be doing the reverse—using the working conditions formerly prevalent in those sectors to energize manufacturing.[2] I describe how the fit between the rhythms of disease and the rhythms of employment affects the ability of persons with disability to maintain employment in any era. In the next chapter, I show how the failure to energize manufacturing increased work disability over time.

Since agricultural workers left for the cities several centuries ago, industrial activities have accounted for the largest share of

---

Alfred Chandler's (1977) *The Visible Hand: The Managerial Revolution in American Business*, which takes a more sympathetic, albeit managerial, perspective, on the development of the modern factory. The description of the new factory derives from Larry Hirschhorn's (1984) *Beyond Mechanization: Work and Technology in a Postindustrial Age*, Shoshana Zuboff's (1988) *In the Age of the Smart Machine: The Future of Work and Power*, Michael Best's (1990) *The New Competition: Institutions of Industrial Restructuring*, William Lazonick's (1990) *Competitive Advantage on the Shop Floor*, Susan Houseman's (1991) *Industrial Restructuring with Job Security: The Case of European Steel*, and Michael Piore and Charles Sabel's (1984) *The Second Industrial Divide: Possibilities for Prosperity*.

[2]The argument that the United States allowed manufacturing to erode needs some amplification. First, the slippage in manufacturing was a relative and gradual phenomenon. It was relative in the sense that manufacturing productivity has continued to increase, but not at the same rate as during the early post–World War II decades. The erosion may be measured best by the difference in the rates at which productivity increased in the United States and its economic competitors, rather than by absolute productivity levels (which are in many cases still higher in the United States). It was gradual in the sense that productivity gains first slowed in the late 1960s, before actually hitting a period of relative stagnation (rising less than 1 percent a year) after the first energy crisis in 1973. Levy (1987, especially chap. 4) describes the productivity dynamics. Second, U.S. manufacturing has had a small renaissance in the last several years (see Nasar 1991a). Fueled by the low value of the dollar, by wages that are either low or competitive relative to other OECD nations, and by the efficiencies gained by reducing the size of the work force in industry, manufacturing has recovered some of the momentum lost in the last two decades. However, some analysts caution that a competitive advantage based on the low value of the dollar and relatively low wages may be difficult to sustain, and that the United States must use this period of recovery to shift to the manufacture of high-quality, high-value added items, which are less likely to be buffeted by international exchange rates. See, for example, Cohen and Zysman 1987, especially chap. 5; and the report of the MIT Commission on Industrial Productivity (Dertouzos, et al., 1989, especially 39–42).

earnings and for most of the growth in the standard of living. The kind of manufacturing may change, and the source of productivity growth may shift among tangible categories, moving first from land to labor, and then to capital, before settling down somewhere in an intangible zone bordered by social organization, services, and human capital. These changes notwithstanding, industry still generates wealth and, sadly, the failure of industry to master new technologies generates impoverishment.[3]

In cycles of innovation, regimentation, and then elimination described by Schumpeter fifty years ago,[4] someone invents a widget, some firm perfects its manufacture and generates a market for it, some other firm learns to make it more cheaply, and the first firm either takes on a new set of activities that generate good profits and high wages or it dies. Schumpeter termed this process *creative destruction,* both to lampoon the notion that an economy is ever in equilibrium and to suggest that the standard of living rises when firms slough off old activities unlikely to generate much profit and add new ones with more growth potential. Americans have never been comfortable with industrialism or its workshop, the modern factory. Most of our visions of utopia hark back to an agricultural past none of us ever knew or suggest a cybernetic future in which machines displace all factory work. Paradoxically, we have always revered the fruits of industrialism, placing great value on what we earn today and on the earnings we project for the future, while reviling the jobs that provide this growth.

Our system of labor relations was built upon this paradox: workers accepted the factory so long as wages were high and kept rising.[5] This had not always been the case. In the early twentieth

---

[3]This set of arguments is spelled out in Cohen and Zysman (1987, especially chap. 2). Cohen and Zysman note that half of GNP derives directly from manufacturing or indirectly from services to manufacturing, and that the standard of living rose with U.S. productivity gains and fell with the slowing of productivity growth, a point reiterated by Levy (1987, 47), using econometric modeling to make his case. However, Cohen and Zysman and Levy echo Schumpeter ([1942] 1950, especially 81) in correlating the standard of living with manufacturing productivity.

[4]Joseph Schumpeter [1942] 1950, especially chap. 7, "The Process of Creative Destruction."

[5]Kai Erickson (1986), in his 1985 presidential address to the American Sociological Association, reviewed the literature on work alienation, noting how the injuries at work permeate nonwork life: "If alienation is a state of

century, before this bargain was struck, the prevailing view was epitomized by Charlie Chaplin's *Modern Times* worker, an innocent lost among the machines, bereft of meaning in work and not yet the recipient of enough money to justify giving up body and soul to the assembly line.

By the mid-twentieth century, popular culture had caught up with the bargain. In "The Life of Riley," William Bendix played a worker in the postwar California aircraft industry, and in "The Honeymooners" Ralph Kramden drove a bus taking men like himself between their apartments and factories. Riley and Kramden, unlike Charlie Chaplin, were no longer lost. They may have detested riveting airplanes or driving a bus, but they had good lives outside their jobs and dreams for the future. Work had become a sideshow, something to endure until real life began after quitting time.

In the 1970s, however, "Take this job and shove it" became an anthem when the value of the paycheck no longer justified the grime and the speedup. This was the era of the Chevrolet Vega fiasco, an attempt by General Motors to increase productivity without compensatory pay increases. This was also the time of Archie Bunker, railing against those who would take a slice of his little pie. Interestingly, Archie abandoned factory work (perhaps we should say it abandoned him), attempting to go it alone as the proprietor of a neighborhood saloon. Microeconomic theory brought to life on the little screen, Archie equilibrated the wages from working for someone else against the risk from opening his own business, choosing the latter as the better deal. A decade later, workers could no longer choose the factory, let alone use high wages to compensate for difficult working conditions. Bruce Springsteen sang about workers displaced from rust belt manufacturing attempting, futilely, to find jobs in the oil refineries of Texas.

Although Daniel Bell never intended *post-industrialism* to mean nonindustrialism, many interpreted the term that way because they wanted to believe that they might finally receive redemption for more than a century of grimy factory work. Others

---

being, it does not reside in the workplace alone, but in the whole of one's existence. . . . [We need to establish how . . . the degradations of the workplace bleed into the larger fabric of one's existence."

used the theory of post-industrialism to legitimate the gradual withdrawal from manufacturing, citing the decline of the factory and the rise of services as evidence of a new, higher level of social development.[6]

Thus, many Americans—intellectuals as well as workers— were glad to let go of manufacturing once the trade-off between the reality of factory work and the dream of increasing wages fell apart. But the real issue is not whether there will be manufacturing, but what kind it will be. The evidence of its importance is too strong and too diverse to come to any other conclusion. Domestically, real wages stagnated as the growth of manufacturing productivity slowed in the early 1970s.[7] Even so, manufacturing still generates a disproportionate amount of earnings and wealth. The expansion of services shifted the earnings distribution, but did not increase the average wage.[8] Internationally, the nations with the fastest increases in real earnings and overall standard of living are those with the fastest growth in manufacturing productivity.[9] Japan and Germany are noted for their manufacturing prowess, not for the growth of their service sectors, even though their service sectors have also grown faster than has the U.S. one. They are certainly not known for their higher tax rates even though these also exceed the U.S. ones, but that is another story.[10]

[6]Fred Block (1990) makes the cogent argument that industrial-era accounting techniques underestimate both the value added from costless improvements in quality and the rise in the standard of living derived from increasing consumption of human services. While it is true that the contemporary economy generates more value than we can readily measure, there is no getting around the fact that people value money earned from work, and that earnings have been relatively stagnant for close to two decades.

[7]See Levy (1987) for the evidence that manufacturing productivity and wages are highly correlated, a point brought up in the report of the MIT Commission on Industrial Productivity (Dertouzous, et al., 1989, especially 39–40 and chap. 2.

[8]See Table 3.7 and accompanying text for these data.

[9]See U.S. Bureau of the Census 1989a, 830–832, table 1429, "Organization for Economic Cooperation and Development (OECD)—Index of Industrial Production, 1975–1987" and table 1430, "Selected Indexes of Manufacturing Activity-Selected Countries: 1970–1987." The latter table measures change in wages denominated in several different ways, but each yielding the same conclusion: that wages are tied to manufacturing productivity changes.

[10]The data on taxes derive from U.S. Bureau of the Census (1989, 827, Table

The media may shape feelings as much as reflect them, so I may be on shaky ground in portraying the changing attitudes of workers through popular culture. In this instance, however, the television shows and popular music tracked the sentiments of workers about as well as social surveys did. Americans tolerated the labor relations of the factory when wages were good and getting better. This is not to say that labor-management conflicts were absent in the 1950s and 1960s, just that these conflicts were bound by a tight set of rules. The system of organizing work was not open for discussion; labor and management merely negotiated how to distribute the fruits of that system.[11]

Using the dictum if it isn't broken, don't fix it, neither workers nor management saw any reason to change the way work itself was done. It wasn't broken: productivity increases allowed real wages to rise by almost half in each decade, enabling government expenditures to rise rather painlessly as well. We didn't fix it: in the shadow of this prosperity, we ignored a substantial body of evidence, some of it dating from the early years of the U.S. factory system,[12] that other ways of organizing work would result in even better productivity gains. More troubling, successful manufacture now seems to require that work be organized differently, suggesting that continuing to rely on the old system of labor relations impedes growth in productivity. In the sections that follow, I describe the traditional U.S. factory system based on the principles of Frederick Taylor and Henry Ford, and the emerging alternative based on the findings of the famous Hawthorne studies. I conclude the chapter by demonstrating that these more participatory forms of work organization redound to the benefit of persons with disabilities by creating a better fit between the rhythms of their medical conditions and the rhythms of work.

Industrial-Strength Work

The Rule

The modern factory emerged in the nineteenth century, when external sources of power were first used to assist production. At

1422, "Percent Distribution of Tax Receipts by Type of Tax, Selected Countries, 1975-1986").

[11]See Osterman 1988, especially chap. 3.

[12]This literature is reviewed in Jones (1990).

that time, power could not be distributed economically, so factories had to be located next to the source of power, the mill situated next to the water wheel being the best example. In these early factories, external sources of power altered craft-based work, making craft workers more efficient, but not replacing them or depriving them of their participation in, if not control over, the production process.[13] Contrary to what many believe, power-assisted craft production never died, surviving relatively intact in such diverse settings as the production of machine tools (the quintessential producer goods industry), furniture, and clothing. In craft-based manufacture, the decision as to how to make things resides, at least partly, in the workers. The machinist sets the lathe, checks the metal to ensure that it has been ground to the correct tolerance, corrects the setting, and then finishes grinding.

But soon after these first factories emerged, managers brought a new set of principles to bear on manufacturing. Production would be designed by those not actually doing the work, and then would be carried out by others.[14] Thus, the labor force was divided into two major camps: those involved in designing how things were to be done, and those doing them. The first group, later to include scientists, engineers, and market and sales personnel as well as managers, was paid on a salaried basis, given flexible job assignments, and given discretion over what they did and how they did it. The second group was told what to do and paid on an hourly basis to do it. It forms the core of workers in the modern industrial factory.[15]

Analysts differ in their explanations of why this system developed, some seeing its origin solely in the technology of production and the search for efficiency,[16] some seeing it as an

[13]The logic of this argument follows Larry Hirschhorn's (1984) *Beyond Mechanization,* especially chap. 1, "Mechanization: The Assembly Line," which describes the shift from craft-based factories to those organized on the principles of what he calls "simple labor," or work divided into as many little tasks as is possible.

[14]Called scientific management to justify design by those not on the line, the field is best known by Frederick Taylor's ([1911] 1967) book of the same name, *The Principles of Scientific Management.*

[15]Osterman (1988, chap. 2) describes the division of labor into these two camps, one accorded autonomy and a salary (very much like my designers category) and the other accorded very few freedoms and paid on a wage basis.

[16]It is difficult to find anyone prior to the human relations school who

attempt to deskill and depower the working class.[17] All agree, however, that this movement to reorganize work had two distinct phases. The first, associated with Frederick Taylor, deconstructed work into a series of separate but potentially connected operations, each of which could be routinized and hence improved. The second, associated with Henry Ford, reconstructed work by conceptualizing an entire process—the whole manufacture—in terms of its routinized parts.[18] To be sure, there was much more to both phases than this summary indicates. Taylorism is often derided for its dehumanizing aspects, but Taylor saw work as a system, albeit a mechanical one, comprising people, machines, and their interactions. Likewise, we may chastise Ford for the conveyor belt that runs the worker, but we must also recognize the assembly line as the nascent stage of continuous-process manufacture, which we rightfully admire for its technical brilliance. Ford also distinguished between the parts of automobile manufacture that could be routinized, which he included in the assembly line, and those that could not, including the making of the individual parts, their storage, and their eventual transportation to the assembly line itself. He systematized what he could, leaving much room for craft work (and a lot of heavy lifting) in all that took place away from the actual assembly point.

However much might be left off the assembly line and thus not subject to Taylor and Ford's system, the factory itself lies at the core of the system. And in this factory, someone figured out how to routinize individual activities to minimize movement (and limit discretion to do things differently) and how to organize these individual activities in the best package, and someone else carried out these instructions. Someone autonomously designed the activities drawing upon time and motion studies and the latest innovations in automated machinery to do so, and someone else

---

believed that there could be any system more efficient than Taylor's factory, and even the human relations school began with the accidental finding that the human group mattered more than the physical environment they were researching, a point explained in much greater depth below. See Homans (1950) for the description of the accidental origins of this school.

[17]This view has been taken by Harry Braverman (1974) and David Noble (1986).

[18]Hirschhorn (1984, especially 9–11) describes the separate contributions of Taylor and Ford in much the same terms.

was asked to do the activities exactly as told. Eventually, as the assembly line grew more sophisticated, Taylor's contribution— the time and motion study—became less important because the system dictated the workers' movements, leaving them even less discretion over their activities.[19]

The factory system assumes that at any one point, there is only one way to do things. Engineers design the assembly line to incorporate this one best way; managers ensure that it runs as designed; and, like a deist's vision of the world, once the foreperson turns on the switch in the morning, it operates without much direction. This has come to be called fixed or batch mode of production because each unit that comes off the assembly line is supposed to be exactly like every other. Indeed, the goal is to design away any chance for variation.

The Hawthorne Exception

To judge by the results of the modern factory, the system developed by Taylor and Ford "worked": productivity increased, eventually even yielding a decent share of income to the workers. However, the Hawthorne studies, initiated during the late 1920s at a Western Electric plant near Chicago, suggest that there never was one best way to do things.[20] These now-famous experiments began on the assumption that one could design a physical environment to improve the physiological aspects of work, in this instance, by measuring the effect of improved lighting on the productivity of workers assembling telephone relays—a logical extension of Taylor's time and motion studies. The researchers found that the lighting did not matter, but that the interactions among workers and between workers and management profoundly altered productivity levels. Moreover, workers retained

[19]See Hirschhorn (1984, 14) on this point.

[20]The Hawthorne experiments were not subjected to statistical analysis until the last decade or so, the conclusion that the "human group" (to use Homans's term) mattered being accepted or rejected on the basis of faith or ideology. In 1978, Richard Franke and James Kaul (1978) used quantitative methods to conclude that human relations mechanisms did not account for productivity differences in the experiments, but that managerial discipline, economic adversity, and other "hard" factors did. Subsequently, articles by Wardwell (1979), Schlaiffer (1980), and Jones (1990) critiqued Franke and Kaul's methods, Jones then reanalyzing the data to find the human relations conclusion of the original research validated.

considerable discretion over their activities even in this most bureaucratized and industrial setting. Therefore, managers had to work hard to create a social environment that would allow this discretion to work to their advantage; workers could as easily use their discretionary powers to retard productivity.

The Hawthorne studies undermined the notion that workers' activities can ever be tied to machines in purely mechanistic ways, thus paving the way for the "human relations" school of management. If the goal was to maximize the number of times the worker turned a ratchet as the cars rolled past, achieving that goal required much more than analyzing the movement of muscle against resistance. However, a more important set of principles emerged from the Hawthorne Studies, principles now used to organize the factories of many successful manufacturers in the United States and, especially, its international competitors.

The New Manufacturing

The traditional factory sought to reduce uncertainty in production by designing the assembly process ahead of time, and by finding the most effective ways of integrating humans into an increasingly mechanized process of manufacture, whether by Taylorist principles or the more sophisticated approach of the human relations school. Designed to be right from the start, this was a system built upon a foundation of small tolerances in delivering materials to the assembly line and then moving the materials along as workers and machines interacted.[21] Once designed, the system had little room for improvement and almost no room for flexibility. There was little room for improvement because the tools to make the parts had been designed to make those parts alone, the conveyor to move the parts along had been made to move those parts alone, the machines to assemble those parts had been designed to do that assembly alone, and the workers doing each part of the assembly had been trained to that part alone. There was no room for flexibility because the system took years to design and then implement. Keynesian regulation of the economy proved a must in this

[21]The argument follows Hirschhorn's (1984) *Beyond Mechanization,* especially chapters 2 and 3, "The Relaxation of Constraint" and "The Technical Foundation of Control Systems."

environment, because cycles of change in manufacture were much longer than the periods of boom and bust that preceded the Depression, necessitating reasonably constant levels of demand to justify building the assembly line in the first place.

The new factory, like the old, usually starts with some radical innovation—a new method of moving parts to the point of assembly, a new piece of electronically controlled machinery or a robot or computer, or all of the above.[22] Indeed, most analysts describe the new factory in terms of these new elements. They work. Just-in-time inventory does not idle as many resources. Programmable machine tools can make for quicker re-tooling. Robots can replace the Taylorized worker, simultaneously lowering labor costs and error rates. Each element allows a quicker response to market signals, helping the firm to minimize the impact of bad times and to maximize the profits when economic conditions improve.

However, the real innovation is not that someone puts each of these elements in when starting anew or figures out a good way to combine them ahead of time. Instead, the system allows the elements to be combined in many different ways or even replaced as new technologies, new experience, or new market realities emerge. Thus, the new factory integrates design and implementation, allowing improvements to be made on the fly.[23]

The organization of work is a central part of this flexibility. Most analysts emphasize the diversity of tasks workers perform because the new factories have fewer job classifications.[24] Others note that the sharp divisions among professional, managers, and labor may be severed as engineers test their ideas on the shop floor, workers fine tune the programs controlling each part of the

[22]The MIT Commission on Industrial Productivity report (Dertouzos, et al., 1989) notes that the each of the elements of Japanese manufacture has been imported to U.S. factories and that each works, but that the system as a whole works better than the sum of its elements and U.S. manufacturers have yet to completely implement it because doing so would require abandoning "such features of the mass production system as long runs of standard cars and the prerogative of laying off large numbers of workers. These attachments to the old ways can undermine the implementation of the new system" (48).

[23]This is why Hirschhorn has called the new factory as much a learning as a working environment. See Hirschhorn 1984, especially, chapt. 11.

[24]See, for example, Osterman 1988, 73; Hirschhorn 1984, 164–167; and Zuboff 1988, especially chapt. 8.

manufacturing process, and both become empowered to make changes in what they do and how they do it.[25]

But more important than the diversity of tasks or the relatively less hierarchical structure is that work itself stops being fixed for the life of the factory. Instead, workers are encouraged to learn and to reorganize work on the basis of what they learn. This is where the Hawthorne studies come into play. In the old factory, social organization might affect productivity at the margin, but firms could still be successful without taking social organization into account. In the new factory, pathological social interactions among workers and between workers and management would block any chance for improvement in the manufacturing process, in effect blocking any chance for success in the competitive marketplace.[26] William Lazonick (1990, 22-23) writes:

> The Great Depression destroyed the cooperative labor-management relations that had contributed to the economic success of the 1920s. . . . management erected internal job structures that, after the rise of industrial unionism in the late 1930s, became integral to the collective bargaining process. [This new structure of] labor management relations . . . created incentives for management to continue to invest in skill-displacing technologies and for workers to supply sufficient effort to permit steady growth in real wages alongside high corporate profit levels.
>
> British industry had already learned the lesson, however, that structures of work organization that promote economic development in one era can later become fetters on development when challenged by a more effective mode of value creation. For the United States, that challenge has come from Japan.
>
> Japanese business organizations have been able . . . to integrate shop-floor workers into the process of planning and coordinating the shop-floor division of labor. . . . If U.S. industrial firms hope to match the recent economic successes of their Japanese competitors, then they will have to provide shop-floor workers with the skills required by advanced technological systems, and they will have to build new struc-

[25]Hirschhorn (1984, 162) and Block (1990, 99) both note the blurring between engineers and machinists in the modern factory.

[26]This is the subject of Larry Hirschhorn's (1988) book, *The Workplace Within: Psychodynamics of Organizational Life*. See especially chap. 4, "Social Defenses".

tures of work organization to ensure that workers use these skills to further enterprise goals.[27]

The factory organized for continuous improvement appears in many different environments, encompassing many organizational structures and firms of many sizes, and making many kinds of goods, some new, some that have been around since the Ice Age. The integrated Japanese manufacturing corporation making consumer electronics, autos, steel, and whatever else may be the best-known form. However, the methods of the continuous-improvement factory have been brought to the German machine tool industry, an amalgam of mid-sized firms specializing in this one set of producer goods,[28] and to the Italian garment district, made up of very small firms making high-style, high-quality, one-of-a-kind clothing.[29] These examples, and a few from the United States as well,[30] suggest that the methods may be implemented almost anywhere and in the manufacture of almost anything.

However, the factory organized for continuous improvement requires labor relations fundamentally different from those of the traditional industrial-era factory. In the latter, workers' activities had been designed de novo, and their attention to how things get done was seen as a threat to this design and hence to productivity. In the new factory, workers' attention to the process of manufacture and then their participation in improving that process cease to be a threat and become instead the linchpin of the operation. Getting workers to participate, however, is never an easy task,

[27]Lazonick 1990, 22–23.

[28]See the Report of MIT Commission on Industrial Productivity (Dertouzos, et al., 1987, 106 243–244) for a description of the German machine tool industry.

[29]Cohen and Zysman (1987,188) describe the contemporary Italian garment manufacturing industry and its ability to respond to market signals.

[30]Zuboff (1988, 418–422) describes the extent to which new factory organization has permeated the U.S. factory system, focusing on its ability to use modern information management techniques in production. Hirschhorn (1984, 1988) uses the case study approach to describe American "factories" (some of the sites he describes, such as nuclear power plants and welfare department back offices, are not standard factory settings, although they produce tangible items, in the former case, electrical power, and in the latter, checks).

especially if management has shunned workers' involvement in the past or run its operations solely on Taylorist principles.

We do know some of the changes that have to be made to make the new factory work. Contravening both pessimistic predictions about the advent of computer-controlled production, the new factory did not deskill the work force or render production workers obsolete.[31] Instead, even the best computer programs provide only an abstract outline of what happens on the shop floor. The experienced worker must be there to interpret the digitized and simplified version of what is going on, providing the same kind of reality check that experienced hands always gave to the new worker on the shop floor. Moreover, the monitoring worker must feel that he or she can intervene to change things that go wrong, both for this production run and, if necessary, on a permanent basis. Larry Hirschhorn describes what firms who have successfully implemented continuous-improvement methods have done to get workers to participate in this way.[32] First, they adopt workers' suggestions, providing positive feedback for being involved. In too many instances, quality circles have become gripe sessions, not a real effort to incorporate workers' suggestions. Second, they avoid penalizing workers when suggestions do not work, avoiding any negative feedback for participation. Third, they make a much stronger commitment to

[31]The deskilling argument, made most forcefully by Harry Braverman (1974), argues that automation will simultaneously render jobs devoid of intellectual content and craft and create unemployment. Braverman thus follows Marx directly in arguing that proletarianization is the necessary outcome once capitalist manufacturing takes flight. However, even those who predicted deskilling little more than a decade ago, were surprised to note that skill levels have been upgraded as the professional and managerial ranks expanded and as each occupation demanded higher skill levels with the passage of time. See, for example, Erik Wright's early work on class structure, in which he posited growing proletarianization, albeit in a structure where some deproletarianization might also occur (Wright and Singleman 1982) and his later work, in which he observed "a clear deproletarianization within and across economic sectors" (Wright and Martin 1987).

[32]This discussion of the elements necessary to make the new factory work is set forth in Hirschhorn's (1984) *Beyond Mechanization,* especially on pages 162–169 in chapter 13, "Can It Happen?". In his later book, *The Workplace Within* (Hirschhorn, 1988), in contrast, he emphasizes the stances that impede the successful operation of the new factory; see especially chap. 4, "The Social Defenses."

job security than does the traditional firm, both to give the learn-ing environment a chance to jell and to sever the traditional connection between taking risks and the threat of unemployment.[33]

The Paradox of Employment Trends

It is easy to denigrate the old factory, but it worked better than any system that had preceded it. It is also easy to wax utopian about the new factory, both ignoring the many workers within this setting who still have menial jobs and the many others forced aside when productivity increases result in layoffs. Finally, it is easy to forget that the new factory was built upon the foundation of the old—taking automated assembly as the point of departure— and that both are ideal types: the old factory never stripped the worker of all discretionary powers, and the new one never fully integrates the worker into all aspects of decisionmaking. Nev-ertheless, there are important differences between the Taylor/Ford model and the factory organized around the principles of con-tinuous improvement: the former separates design and implemen-tation and reduces discretion on the shop floor; the latter dampens distinctions between management and labor in order to get both involved in both design and implementation.

Labor market analysts target the factory for study because of its importance in determining the overall standard of living and because it has defined labor relations for the other sectors of the economy. Thus, when manufacturing firms separated workers into two groups, one given discretion over working conditions, more secure employment, higher pay, and a salary, the other given highly defined jobs, employment subject to prevailing economic conditions, and an hourly wage, nonmanufacturing firms were quick to adopt this scheme. The university may be the best exam-ple of this phenomenon. Touted as the quintessential service organization, the university nevertheless divides its employees in exactly the same way as did an automobile factory in the 1930s. Professionals, in this case the professoriat, and managers, in this

[33]Many authors have emphasized the importance of job security in making the social forces in the workplace cohesive. See, for example, Rothschild and Whitt 1986, especially chap. 7, 160–167; Osterman 1988, especially 70–75; Cole 1979, especially chap. 1; and Lazonick 1990, 288–298.

case the administration, are accorded one set of rules; staff—meaning anyone else—another.

Regardless of whether this system of organizing labor made sense for the factory when the modern factory evolved early in this century, and regardless of whether it made sense to graft the system onto nonmanufacturing organizations later, the changes in the economy over the last two decades ought to have expanded the proportion of the labor force working under the more benign conditions traditionally assigned to salaried workers. After all, the share of workers in occupations traditionally given salaried employment grew by more than a quarter, and these workers were much likelier to be in the kinds of firms—finance, business, and professional services—where salaried employment predominates.[34] Instead, the terms of employment for many professionals and managers came to resemble the conditions traditionally assigned to those on the assembly line.[35] Job security became a thing of the past, tasks were narrowed and routinized, and benefits and pay were rescinded, enabling some analysts to claim that the current recession heralded the fall of the middle manager. Thus, when one could make a good argument that we should be extending the conditions of salaried employment to production workers in manufacturing, we did the reverse, extending the rigid work rules of the old assembly line to the ranks of the managerial and professional employee.

The Rhythms of Disability, the Rhythms of Work

The assembly line in the traditional factory was a place of small tolerances. If the part did not get to the conveyor by the time the frame rolled by, if someone noticed that the part had a flaw when the frame arrived and had to wait for the next part, or if the worker did not have time to attach the part to the frame, the entire assembly of this and every other widget had to stop. Each action of the assembly process had to be timed and coordinated. To do this, experienced workers were observed under conditions believed to

[34]See Tables 4.1 and 4.2.

[35]In Chapter 4, I told this story using data consistent with the theory that contingent employment arrangements are expanding. However, many authors, most notably Osterman, have made this point explicitly. See Osterman 1988, 77–79; see also Mansnerus 1991; and Belous 1989.

the similar to those on the "real line," and the "real line" would be built on the expectation that able-bodied workers could be found and would perform as tested in the laboratory. This left little room for persons with disabilities, primarily because they could not meet the performance standards built into the line. A job requires lifting the part onto the frame; arthritis limits the individual's ability to lift. Another job requires the worker to run a part across the floor from a storage bin to the conveyor; asthma limits the number of times the worker can do this. A third job requires precision crafting of a tool; an injury to the hand prevents the worker from grabbing the calibrator.

It is not hard to see that the physical demands of much factory work, indeed, of most traditional blue-collar work, would preclude the hiring of persons with disabilities. And yet the onset of many of the chronic conditions that are common causes of work disability comes late in life, well after workers have been in their jobs for years. Arthritis, heart and lung disease, and neurological conditions typically appear when workers are in their 40s and 50s. Unlike trauma, these chronic conditions often have a subtle onset, sometimes not being noticed for several years, other times never bothering the worker enough to require medical care. During this long prodromal phase, workers may complain to their colleagues about the condition once in a while without actually taking any time off because of it. As the condition gradually worsens, they may make slight adjustments to their work activities, adjustments even their colleagues (and sometimes they themselves) may not notice. A crafts worker with arthritis in the right hand may use the left to assist in turning the wrench; an assembler with a back problem may develop stronger wrist muscles to compensate for this condition.

Persons with disabilities trying to get a first job and those who have had to suspend their careers after an illness or injury often have a tough time finding work. However, most persons who develop disabilities due to chronic conditions never leave their jobs, and many others do so only for short periods. Indeed, only when someone has a very severe impairment that fits poorly with a very physically demanding job will physical disability preclude staying at work. We know this to be so because disability rates among laborers with impairments were once much lower than they are now—20 percent lower—even though their jobs have become less physically demanding. Not only has automation made physically demanding jobs less taxing than they used to be, but fewer workers have physically demanding work. Even so, work disability rates continue to rise.

The assembly line is physically demanding, but this is not why it proved inhospitable to the person with disabilities. What makes the assembly line—and any industry that organizes work the same way—problematic for the person with disabilities is that its rigid work rules and time requirements do not mesh well with the rhythms of chronic disease. Most chronic conditions fluctuate both within the day and over a longer period of time. The person with arthritis experiences morning stiffness on a daily basis, and also has alternating periods of flareups and remissions lasting weeks, months, or even years. The person with asthma may do quite well over the winter, but usually suffers as spring pollen and summer pollution come along. The person with cancer may have to lie low when undergoing chemotherapy, but will spring back afterwards. Even HIV-related conditions are cyclical, acute infections and periods of night sweats, fever, and exhaustion alternating with periods when the illness is relatively quiescent.

People with chronic conditions try to accommodate to these rhythms by fitting work and family responsibilities around episodes of illness. They will husband their energy when their conditions require them to rest or get medical attention, but will work especially hard when symptoms abate. The rigid work rules of the assembly line may not preclude these kinds of accommodations, but they make them more difficult. Getting to work by seven when experiencing morning stiffness, pushing to do more work during the spring when asthma flares, maintaining a set schedule while undergoing cancer treatment—these problems, rather than the brute force requirements of jobs, are the impediments faced by the person with a disability. On the other hand, workers who have discretion over the pace and scheduling of their jobs are much less likely to stop working after onset of illness, precisely because they are able to mesh the rhythms of work and the rhythms of their medical conditions. This relationship holds across illnesses, industries, and the physical demands of jobs. It holds across levels of the workplace hierarchy, across levels of satisfaction with the specific job, and across levels of commitment to persevere in work of any kind. All else being equal, people with discretion over work activities will be less likely to stop working whether they have severe heart disease or mild back pain, whether they are employed in an auto plant or university, whether they are common laborers or nuclear physicists, whether they love their jobs or hate them, and whether they want to continue working or cannot wait to retire.[36]

The Paradox Comes Home to Roost

More than six decades have passed since the Hawthorne experiments showed that workers retain considerable discretion over work, even in jobs subjected to the most thorough time and motion studies, and that this discretion could be put to good as well as bad uses. More than three decades have passed since economists first noticed that increases in productivity come from such intangibles as the way work is organized, the kinds of services provided, and the human capital workers bring to employment,[37] again suggesting that how people interact plays a key role in determining the extent of a society's wealth. More than a decade has passed since the structure of the factory organized around the principles of continuous improvement was described, showing that integrating the worker into the decisionmaking on the shop floor is essential to the success of manufacturing.[38] Now we also

[36]I developed this model of work disability during my years as a researcher with the UCSF Multipurpose Arthritis Center, the various forms of arthritis being the leading cause of lost work. Starting with group discussions with persons with rheumatoid arthritis (essentially using case studies to develop the model), I proceeded to cross-sectional and then longitudinal studies of work disability among persons with this illness, and then to longitudinal studies of persons with cancer, asthma, and HIV-related illnesses, and econometric modeling of federal surveys of persons with a broad range of chronic conditions (Yelin, Nevitt, and Epstein 1980; Yelin, et al., 1980; Yelin 1986, 1991; Yelin, Henke, and Epstein 1986, 1987; Blanc and Yelin 1991; Greenwald, et al. 1989). Subsequently, the findings of the rheumatoid arthritis studies have been corroborated by others researching this illness (Reisine et al. 1989), and by those looking into the causes of work disability among persons with cardiovascular conditions (Murphy 1991).

[37]See Solow (1957) for the first suggestion of this relationship and Denison (1974) for a more thorough discussion. Solow's work underlies the theory of post-industrialism espoused by Daniel Bell (1973), which was reviewed in Chapter 4.

[38]See, for example, Cole 1979, especially 240–250. Cole argues that the

know that the social organization of work affects the work disability rate. Thus, we have a lot of evidence that participatory work environments redound to the benefit of the worker in terms of job satisfaction and lowered rates of disability, to the benefit of the firm in terms of profits, and to the benefit of the society in terms of the standard of living. Finally, we know that job security is essential to make the participatory work environment jell. Given all this, it is all the more amazing that we have chosen to let the working conditions of the old factory expand within manufacturing and outside of it and to make contingent employment the rule rather than the exception. It would appear to a neutral observer that we are willing to forgo higher rates of economic growth—less money for all of us—either because we fear that relaxing the rhythms of the Taylorized factory will unfetter the worker from all discipline, unleashing a wave of malingering in the process, or because management is unconvinced or unwilling to be convinced that participatory work styles are essential to increased productivity in the new manufacturing, the accumulating evidence from Japan, Germany, France, and Italy notwithstanding.

So far, I have suggested that the success of the manufacturing sector (and hence of the economy at large) cannot be separated from the working conditions within that sector and that the working conditions within manufacturing cannot be separated from the work disability problem. It is now time to add the third leg of the triangle by showing that the work disability problem can not be separated from the success of the manufacturing sector.

---

participatory style of the working conditions, rather than an inherent commitment to work or the firm, accounts for the higher rate of productivity growth in Japan relative to the United States.

6

Work Disability and the Transformation of the Labor Force

The labor market has been acting in very strange ways over the last two decades, shifting away from manufacturing employment while shifting toward manufacturing-type working conditions, bringing millions of women, especially younger women, into work, but taking millions of men, especially older men, out of it. Analysis of labor market data demonstrates that the participation of persons with disabilities in the labor force is tied to these more general labor market trends.[1]

[1]The evidence for this argument derives from the analysis of eighteen years of National Health Interview Survey data that I have completed with my colleague, Dr. Patricia P. Katz. The National Health Interview Survey asks about 110,000 individuals each year to report their health status, including their labor force participation. It is designed so that one can make inferences about the population living in the community in the continental United States; it does not collect information from persons in the armed forces or in institutions. The latter omission reduces estimates of the impact of illness on work, since, by definition, persons in institutions are not employed in the competitive economy. However, since a majority of them are over 65, the effect is minimal. Dr. Katz and I have published several papers based on this database, which discuss the technical issues involved in using the National Health Interview Survey for labor market studies. Rather than repeat these discussions, I refer the reader to Yelin (1989); Yelin and Katz (1990), which uses the Longitudinal Study of Aging, an offshoot of the Health Interview Survey; Yelin (1991); and Yelin and Katz (1991). The main limitation, as with any survey, is that although the sample size of the National Health Interview is large, it is not large enough to have much confidence in estimates for any one year. Instead, I look to make my case by finding consistent results using different estimation techniques, and by relying on long-term, rather than one-

The notion that the employment prospects of persons with disabilities—like those of other groups suffering discrimination, particularly nonwhites and women—cannot be separated from

---

year changes.

This chapter reports the results of the statistical analysis, albeit in truncated and simplified form. To highlight how the transformation in the labor force affects persons with disabilities, I have selected three crucial years from among the eighteen in the database. The year 1970 preceded the onset of the energy crisis by three years and, in the view of many, represents the high point of the U.S. economy, since the 1960s were the last period when the standard of living increased consistently and dramatically. The year 1982, in contrast, saw the highest unemployment rate in the post–World War II period and was the low point in the longest and most severe recession in the last five decades. By 1987, the third year selected for study, the United States had sustained over five consecutive years of economic expansion, and the labor force participation rate had hit an all-time high (it was especially high compared to those of the country's European competitors). Taking three years randomly from among the eighteen would reduce the natural variance from the time series; taking three years nonrandomly on the basis of their contrasting economic situations accentuates the time trend I am trying to demonstrate. Tables 6.5 through 6.7 present the results of regressions using all eighteen years of data. In these regressions, I am testing the effect of change in an industry's employment on the change in its disabled employment.

I use three measures of change in employment and disabled employment within industries: the absolute change between years (one year's total employment minus the previous year's total); percent change between years (one year's total employment divided by the previous year's totals), and share change (an industry's share of all employment in one year minus that industry's share in the previous one). Absolute change represents real hiring and real withdrawal from the labor force, but this measure is constrained somewhat by the size of the industries doing the expansion or contraction, since small industries can never hire a large number of workers relative to big ones. Percent change indicates speed of growth or retrenchment, but, in contrast, does not measure real hiring or retrenchment, since an absolute change of a few thousand workers can result in a big percentage change in a small industry, even if relatively few workers actually find a job. Share change captures the shift among industries, but, again, an industry's share of employment can wax or wane without anyone's being hired or laid off, since an industry with a million workers in every year would have lost its share of employment merely because the size of the overall labor market grew. Nevertheless, share change comes closest to tracking real change in an industry's health, at least as far as employment is concerned, since it is not dependent on the size of the industry. In the regressions, I test several sets of models. The simplest case—change between pairs of years in employment of disabled persons in an industry regressed on change in overall employment in that industry—proved to have a better fit than lagged and lead models for all three measures of change, suggesting that any adjustment to change in the employ-the overall employment situation is neither new nor novel. After all, the passage of the Social Security Disability Insurance (SSDI) program was delayed for several decades out of the fear that disability compensation would become a costly alternative to welfare for the unemployed.[2] Much later, federal civil rights legislation barred discrimination in employment on the basis of race, sex,and disability, using labor market data as evidence that these groups did not participate as fully in employment as they might.[3] However, in all these discussions, discrimination in employment was thought to course evenly through the labor force. I am suggesting a much more specific tie between the transformation of the labor force and employment among persons with disabilities. Thus, while it is true that older men are vanishing from all sectors of the economy, they are vanishing disproportionately from vanishing industries and occupations. Older men with disabilities are the leading edge of this phenomenon, vanishing from vanishing sectors faster than are such men without disabilities. And while it is also true that young and middle-aged women are entering all sectors of the economy, they are entering the rising ones faster. Younger women with disabilities benefit from this trend, entering the rising sectors of the economy which need their labor.[4] Thus, I

---

ment picture affecting persons with disabilities occurs within the same year (this should not be unexpected, since a year is a long time in labor market cycles). However, I also estimated a pure lag model, in which the change in an industry's employment results in change in employment for persons with disabilities one year later; a pure lead model, in which the change in disabled employment occurs one year before expansion or contraction within industries; and a lag-lead model, in which persons with disabilities leave contracting industries a year before other persons and enter expanding ones a year after other persons. Finally, I tested the additional impact of the aging of the population and the growth in the proportion of the population with activity limitation due to chronic disease on each of these models.

[2]See, for example, Berkowitz (1987, 43–49) for a history of the passage of Social Security Disability Insurance.

[3]Yelin (1991) both provides an example of such an analysis and cites previous ones.

[4]As I will show later, there is no evidence to support the notion that work disability lags behind expansions in employment in the rising sectors of the economy in the sense that it follows them in time and only weak evidence that it leads contractions in employment in declining ones in the sense that it precedes them in time. Thus, I am not using the terms leading and following to connote ordering of events in time, just disproportionate effects.

Table 6.1. Change in U.S. Labor Force Participation Rates among Men by Race, Age, and Limitation Status, 1970–1972 versus 1985–1987

Race	Age group	Change in % working	Change in % limited and working	Change in % not limited and working
White	18–44	1	–6	2
	45–54	–2	–12	–1
	55–64	–16	–26	–13
	Total	–1	–13	–1
Nonwhite	18–44	–5	–18	–4
	45–54	–5	–18	–3
	55–64	–22	–30	–18
	Total	–6	–21	–6
All	18–44	1	–8	0
	45–54	–3	–15	–1
	55–64	–17	–27	–13
	Total	–2	–14	–2

Source: Author's analysis of 1970–1987 National Health Interview Survey data.

argue that persons with disabilities played a central role in the transformation from an older, masculine, manufacturing labor force to a younger, feminine, service-based one, first showing that disability, like race, exaggerates overall labor market trends, and then showing that persons with disabilities experienced a disproportionate amount of displacement from declining industries and less than a proportionate increase in expanding ones.

Sex, Race, and the Labor Market

Getting and retaining jobs, especially good ones, is an inherently discriminatory process. Employers select on the basis of justifiable differences in skills, experience, and formal training, and on the basis of unjustifiable biases about race, sex, and disability status. (There is much good evidence that job-related differences do not account for the labor market experience of minorities, women, and person with disabilities, so much, in fact, that a footnote documenting this assertion would constitute a lengthy book.) To a lesser extent, workers choose to enter the labor force and then choose among employers, using their own sets of justifiable and unjustifiable criteria.[5] Through a process accommodating these dual queues, patterns of labor force participation get established. Most working-age men have always worked; most still do, though older men have been withdrawing from work in increasing numbers over the last two decades. The era of Rosie the Riveter notwithstanding, most women stayed out of the labor force once they got married, a situation that has changed dramatically now that young women are entering the labor force in record numbers.

The rise in women's labor force participation and the fall in older men's have led many analysts to claim that sex discrimination in employment, if not in pay, may be waning. There is good reason, however, to believe otherwise, since in general the professions women have entered have not been those from which men have exited, and even when significant numbers of women have entered traditionally male professions, men have abandoned

[5]This description of how workers choose employers and vice versa derives from Reskin and Roos (1990, especially chap. 2).

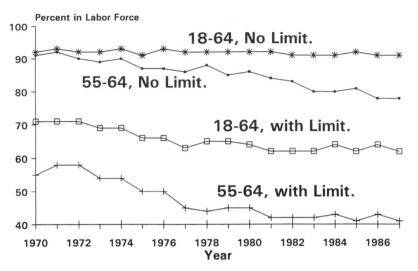

Fig. 6.1   Labor Force Participation of White Men by Age and Limitation, U.S., 1970–1987

Source: Author's analysis of National Health Interview Survey data.

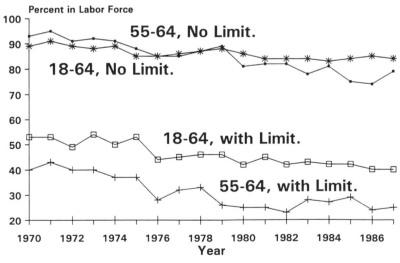

Fig. 6.2   Labor Force Participation of Nonwhite Men by Age and Limitation, U.S., 1970–1987

Source: Author's analysis of National Health Interview Survey data.

Table 6.2. Change in U.S. Labor Force Participation Rates among Women by Race, Age, and Limitation Status, 1970–1972 versus 1985–1987

Race	Age group	Change in % working	Change in % limited and working	Change in % not limited and working
White	18–44	41	41	41
	45–54	29	23	29
	55–64	0	−8	4
	Total	32	20	35
Nonwhite	18–44	15	10	15
	45–54	8	−14	13
	55–64	−6	−26	2
	Total	12	−6	13
All	18–44	37	37	37
	45–54	24	17	28
	55–64	0	−8	4
	Total	29	21	32

Source: Author's analysis of 1970–1987 National Health Interview Survey data.

those sectors or women have entered different subspecialties, leaving a discrimination that is much subtler and harder to detect.[6] For example, older men left manufacturing, and by and large, women entered services. When women entered the residential real estate field, men left for the more highly remunerated commercial side. When women feminized medicine as a whole, they did so by entering a few specialties, such as pediatrics, leaving others, such as surgery, largely the province of men. Nevertheless, the overall labor market was feminized, mostly by the entrance of younger women and the exit of older men.

Racial discrimination abetted this transformation. Between 1970 and 1987, labor force participation among all working-age white men fell by a scant 1 percent, far less than the 6 percent decline among all working-age nonwhite men (Table 6.1 and Figures 6.1 and 6.2).[7] Not surprisingly, older nonwhite men, whose labor force participation rate has always been lower than that among white men of similar age, experienced a disproportionate falloff, the decline in their labor force participation exceeding that of white men by more than a third. However, young nonwhite men also saw their employment prospects worsen (their labor force participation rates declined 5 percent in relative terms), while labor force participation among young white men increased, albeit only slightly, by 1 percent. Overall, the feminization of the workforce hardly affected the labor force participation of white men, and to the extent it did, only those aged 55–64 experienced a substantial falloff in employment. Nonwhite men of all ages, however, lost ground, and the falloff reached 22 percent among nonwhite men aged 55–64.

Nonwhite women did not share in the employment gains experienced by white women, especially by young white women (Table 6.2 and Figures 6.3 and 6.4). However, since nonwhite women have always had to work, white women's disproportionate gains resulted in roughly equal labor force participation rates. Between 1970 and 1987, labor force participation of all working-age white

---

[6]Ibid. 10–16.

[7]Figures 6.1 through 6.4 show the labor force participation rate of white and nonwhite men and women for the years 1970 through 1987, stratified by age and disability status. Tables 6.1 and 6.3 show changes in labor force participation rates between the first and last three-year periods under study; three-year averages provide more reliable estimates of these changes.

Fig. 6.3 Labor Force Participation of White Women by Age and Limitation, U.S., 1970–1987
Source: Author's analysis of National Health Interview Survey data.

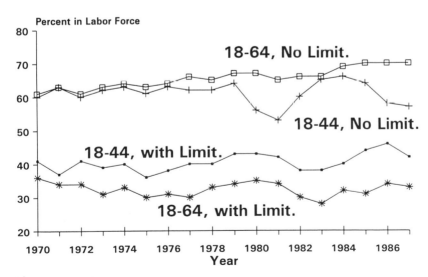

Fig. 6.4 Labor Force Participation of Nonwhite Women by Age and Limitation, U.S., 1970–1987
Source: Author's analysis of National Health Interview Survey data.

women surged 32 percent; that of nonwhite women grew 12 percent, a substantial, albeit smaller, gain. All the gains for white women occurred among those aged 18–44 and 45–54; the labor force participation rate among white women aged 55–64 stagnated after 1970 (it had increased substantially in the 1960s as some mothers of baby boomers returned to the labor force after their children grew up). Nonwhite women aged 55–64, in contrast, saw their labor force participation rate fall by 6 percent after 1970; most of these women had been in the labor force for several decades.

Triple Jeopardy

Disability makes a bad situation worse, accentuating racial and age differences in labor force trends by hastening the withdrawal of older men from the labor force, especially older nonwhite men, and slowing the entrance of women, especially young nonwhite women.

Thus, while labor force participation hardly changed among all working-age white men between 1970 and 1987, falling by 1 percent, as noted above, working-age white men with disabilities experienced a 13 percent decline in labor force participation (Figure 6.1 and Table 6.1). Indeed, while white men without disabilities at the beginning and middle of their careers held their ground, the same cannot be said of those with disabilities, whose labor force participation rates fell by 6 percent among those aged 18–44 and by 12 percent among those aged 45–54. Older white men with disabilities fared the poorest of all, their labor force participation rate falling 26 percent in relative terms, from a very low 1970 base of 55 percent.

Nonwhite men with disabilities fell farther and from a much lower starting point than did whites (Figure 6.2 and Table 6.1). After sustaining a 21 percent decline between 1970 and 1987, fewer than half of nonwhite men of working ages with disabilities remained in the labor force by the latter year. In contrast to whites, young nonwhite men with disabilities also saw substantial declines in labor market opportunities, their participation rate falling by 18 percent. But it is the work experience of older nonwhite men that highlights the role disability status plays in overall labor market dynamics. Nonwhite men aged 55–64 with disabilities experienced a 30 percent falloff in their already low labor force participation rates, a decline 15 percent greater than that among white men of these ages with disabilities, two-thirds greater than that among nonwhite men of these ages without disabilities, and more than twice as great as that among white men of these ages without disabilities.

Regardless of race, however, men with disabilities fared poorly in overall labor market dynamics. When labor force participation rates stagnated among young men without disabilities, young men with disabilities sustained a substantial decline; when middle-aged men without disabilities saw their labor force participation rate decline by a scant 1 percent, those with disabilities experienced a 15 percent fall; when older men without disabilities withdrew from work, those with disabilities did so at twice the rate. Summed across men of all working ages, the feminization of the labor force has hardly taken any toll on those without disabilities, their participation rate falling by only 2 percent between 1970 and 1987, one-seventh the decline among those with disabilities. To highlight this disproportionate impact, I apportioned lost job opportunities to men with and without disabilities. If men's overall labor force participation had not declined between 1970 and 1987, about 1.4 million more men would have been working in the latter year. Men with disabilities, representing 14 percent of all working-age men, account for 60 percent of these lost opportunities.

The services boom of the 1980s carried many young white women with disabilities into the labor force (Figure 6.3 and Table 6.2). Indeed, the demand for such workers was so strong that the labor force participation rate of white women aged 18–44 with disabilities increased by the same percentage as that for those without disabilities (41 percent), albeit from a lower base (39 versus 51 percent, respectively). However, older white women with disabilities did not share proportionally in the employment gains of those without disabilities. White women aged 45–54 with disabilities experienced a 23 percent increase in labor force participation, far smaller than the increase among such women without disabilities. White women aged 55–64 with disabilities saw their labor force participation rate fall even though the proportion of such women without disabilities in the labor force was still increasing, albeit by a scant 4 percent. Among white women with disabilities of all working ages, labor force participation rose by 20 percent, a substantial rise but one 45 percent smaller than that experienced by white women without disabilities.

Nonwhite women with disabilities fared more poorly (Figure 6.4 and Table 6.2). Young nonwhite women with disabilities did not experience the employment gains of those without disabilities, let alone those experienced by white women. And nonwhite women aged 45–54 and 55–64 with disabilities sustained a substantial falloff in labor force participation, even while the proportion of such women without disabilities in the labor force was still rising. Overall, the losses among the latter two groups of nonwhite women with disabilities were far greater than the gains among those aged 18–44, driving down the overall labor force participation rate among nonwhite women with disabilities by 6 percent—and this occurred while the proportion of all nonwhite women in the labor force expanded by 12 percent.

A dramatically expanding labor market pulled women with disabilities into the labor force: the labor force participation rate among all working-age women with disabilities increased by 21 percent in relative terms, from 34 to 41 percent (Table 6.2). As great as this advance was, it pales in comparison to the increased employment of women without disabilities. By 1987, close to 12 million more women were working than would have been had labor force participation rates not increased after 1970, but only about 650,000 more women with disabilities were in the labor force in 1987 than in 1970. Representing 15 percent of all women, women with disabilities received only 6 percent of the new jobs.

Work Disability and the Vanishing Older Worker

The U.S. economy, for all its faults, has incorporated the baby boom generation into the labor force, belying the notion that there is a natural limit to the proportion of the population that can be accommodated with jobs (Table 6.3). Between 1970 and 1987, labor force participation among all working-age persons increased 10 percent. While this massive expansion of the overall labor force was occurring, middle-aged and older persons with disabilities were left out, and young persons with disabilities did not share equally in the gains of their generation, their labor force participation rate increasing by 5 percent while young persons without disabilities experienced a 16 percent increase. Overall, then, the

Table 6.3. Change in U.S. Labor Force Participation Rates among
Working-Age People by Age and Limitation Status,
1970–1972 versus 1985–1987

Age group	Change in % working	Change in % limited and working	Change in % not limited and working
18–44	14	5	16
45–54	10	−6	11
55–64	−10	−27	−6
Total	10	−4	13

Source: Author's analysis of 1970–1987 National Health Interview Survey data.

10 percent increase in the labor force participation rate among all working-age persons represented the net effect of a 13 percent increase among those without disabilities and a 4 percent decline among those with disabilities.

"The Great American Jobs Machine" proved very selective in those it benefited. Mid-career persons without disabilities saw their labor force participation rates increase, while such persons with disabilities sustained a 6 percent decline. All older workers experienced worsened job prospects, but those with disabilities were especially vulnerable, their labor force participation rates falling 27 percent between 1970 and 1987, four times as great a decline as that among older workers without disabilities.

Thus, all older workers are vanishing, but those with disabilities are doing so faster. Had 1970 labor force participation rates among older workers continued until 1987, an additional 1.3 million persons aged 55–64 would have had jobs. Persons of 55 to 64 with disabilities, representing 29 percent of all 55 to 64 year-olds, accounted for 53 percent of these lost job opportunities. Disability plays a central role in labor market dynamics, clearing many older workers from the labor force while assisting a few younger ones in finding work. In the next section, I show that this trend is tied to the transformation from a manufacturing to a service economy.

The Rubber Band

In the early 1980s, labor market politics made page one. The problems of workers displaced from manufacturing during the recession, particularly in the Midwest and Northeast, garnered the most attention. Millions of people who had worked in factories for their entire careers lost their jobs or feared that they would soon do so. A debate raged between those arguing that the problems of manufacturing could be solved by letting the market equilibrate employment and wage levels (rather than having union contracts and government regulations perform this role) and those arguing for greater state intervention on behalf of beleaguered industries and their beleaguered employees. The debate about work disability echoed these themes, one side holding that state intervention, specifically, the growth of disability compensation programs, bred the problem, the other arguing that growing state intervention reflected the growing medical need of an aging work force.

With the election of Ronald Reagan, the free market side gained the upper hand in policy matters. And so in a matter of months, the magnitude of disability benefits was reduced, and several hundred thousand SSDI recipients had their benefits terminated in the belief that their medical conditions had improved sufficiently to allow a return to work. These were not popular actions. Most Americans knew someone whose SSDI benefits were taken away, and most were unwilling to accept the charge that these former SSDI recipients were malingerers.

In the intervening years, we have developed more subtle mechanisms to accommodate change in the labor force. Rather than the shock therapy of massive unemployment, which accompanied the recession of the early 1980s, we accommodate the need to shift workers among industries and lower the overall costs of compensation by using contingent forms of employment, taking a little from many workers year after year rather than taking it all from a few workers all at one time. As part of this accommodation, the rubber band propels large numbers of older workers away from manufacturing and brings millions of younger ones to service industries. The early pension, the golden handshake, and the ability to claim Social Security benefits at age 62 cushion the loss of income for older workers; the lack of these mechanisms forces more of the young into the labor force.

However, the rubber band is wound more tightly around workers with disabilities, propelling greater proportions of older workers with disabilities away from declining industries, while

Table 6.4. Correlation between Change in an Industry's Total Employment and Change in Its Employment of Persons with Activity Limitations among U.S. Industries by Age, 1970–1987

Measure of change	Age group	1970–82	1982–87	1970–87
Absolute	All	.96	.89	.96
	18–44	.91	.94	.96
	55–64	.20	.77	.50
%	All	.41	.88	.97
	18–44	−.09	.78	.55
	55–64	.77	.98	.96
Share	All	.79	.96	.92
	18–44	.61	.94	.87
	55–64	.02	.53	.92

Source: Author's analysis of 1970–1987 National Health Interview Survey data.

bringing fewer with disabilities into the ascending ones. Table 6.4 summarizes this dynamic; Tables 6.5 through 6.7 provide greater detail on the exact mechanisms at work. By any measure, employment among persons with disabilities is tightly linked to overall employment trends in specific industries: the correlations between change in employment among working-age persons with disabilities in a given industry and change in employment among all working-age persons in the same industry for the period 1970–1987 range from .92 (share change) to .97 (percent change) (Table 6.4). Moreover, for both young and old workers, the correlation between employment among persons with disabilities in an industry and the industry's overall employment levels grew stronger with time, suggesting that the rubber band became tighter with the passage of time (Table 6.4). Thus, not only are workers with disabilities dependent upon more general employment trends, but they are growing more dependent as the years unfold. In Chapter 4, I described how the modern firm has come to use its labor force as another element in the just-in-time inventory. The regression analysis summarized in Tables 6.5 through 6.7 suggests that employment among persons with disabilities responds very quickly to changes in the demand for labor. For each measure, I estimated regression models in which employment among persons with disabilities lagged one year behind changes in an industry's

Table 6.5. Regression Results: Effect of Absolute Change in an Industry's Employment on the Absolute Change in Its Employment of Workers with Disabilities between Pairs of Years among U.S. Industries, 1970–1987

Dependent variable	Main independent variable	Other independent variables	% of variance explained
Change in disabled employment	Change in employment		12
Change in disabled employment	Change in employment	Age distribution[a] % with Activity limitation, by age[b]	24
Change in disabled employment, one year later	Change in employment		1
Change in disabled employment, one year later/earlier	Change in employment		4
Change in disabled employment, one year earlier	Change in employment		2

Source: Author's analysis of 1970–1987 National Health Interview Survey data.

Notes: The "Age distribution" variable is the percentage of the working-age population in each age group. The "% with Activity limitation" variable is the percentage with activity limitation in each age group. In the "one year later" model, a change in an industry's employment affects that industry's employment of persons with activity limitations one year later. In the "one year later/earlier" model, persons with disabilities leave contracting industries one year before employment in an industry as a whole contracts and enter expanding industries one year after the industry as a whole expands. In the "one year earlier" model, a change in an industry's employment of persons with disabilities occurs one year before the employment in the industry as a whole changes.

[a]$p < .05$ for age group 45–54; n.s. for age groups 18–44 and 55–64.

[b]n.s.

Table 6.6. Regression Results: Effect of Percent Change in an Industry's Employment on the Percent Change in Its Employment of Workers with Disabilities between Pairs of Years among U.S. Industries, 1970–1987

Dependent variable	Main independent variable	Other independent variables	% of variance explained
% Change in disabled employment	% Change in employment		55
% Change in disabled employment	% Change in employment	Age distribution[a] % with Activity limitation, by age[b]	2
% Change in disabled employment, one year later	% Change in employment		1
% Change in disabled employment, one year later/ earlier	% Change in employment		0
% Change in disabled employment, one year earlier	% Change in employment		3

Source and notes: Same as Table 6.5.

[a]n.s.

[b]n.s.

Table 6.7. Regression Results: Effect of Change in an Industry's Share of Total Employment on the Change in Its Share of Employment of Workers with Disabilities between Pairs of Years among U.S. Industries, 1970–1987

Dependent variable	Main independent variable	Other independent variables	% of variance explained
Change in share of disabled employment	Change in share of employment		93
Change in share of disabled employment	Change in share of employment	Age distribution[a] % with Activity limitation, by age[b]	96
Change in share of disabled employment, one year later	Change in share of employment		24
Change in share of disabled employment, one year later/ earlier	Change in share of employment		37
Change in share of disabled employment, one year earlier	Change in share of employment		23

Source and notes: Same as Table 6.5.

[a]n.s.

[b]n.s.

employment, led it by one year, or led it by a year if the industry was shedding workers ("first fired") and lagged it by a year if the industry was expanding ("last hired"). In every instance, however, the models in which employment among disabled persons responded in the same year to changes in overall employment in an industry achieved a better fit than did the time-dependent ones. Persons with disabilities are a part of just-in-time inventory.[8]

The rubber band can react very quickly to the shifting demand for labor. Manufacturing employment grew absolutely between 1970 and 1982, even while its share of all employment was declining. Reflecting this mixed picture, the proportion of all manufacturing workers with disabilities declined very slightly, from 9.0 to 8.9 percent (or by about 1 percent). After 1982, manufacturing employment was in a free-fall, and employment among manufacturing workers with disabilities declined precipitously, three times as fast as among those without disabilities (even though manufacturing employment among workers without disabilities was declining rapidly, too). Meanwhile, the rubber band brought several million persons with disabilities into the booming service industries, raising the proportion of all service industry workers with disabilities from 9.8 to 11.6 percent between 1970 and 1987. Ever sensitive to shifting winds, the proportion of government workers with disabilities increased dramatically as overall government employment expanded during the 1970s, but then retreated after the Reagan era cuts in government took hold in the following years, falling from 10.2 percent of all government workers in 1982 to 9.4 percent in 1987, or by about 8 percent in relative terms.

Not all industries fit the overall patterns this well. But enough

---

[8]Tables 6.5 through 6.7 also test the notion that employment among persons with disabilities responds to the change in the proportions of the working-age population aged 45–54 and 55–64 (the theory that baby boomers will crowd out older workers) and to the change in the proportions of persons these ages with activity limitation (the theory that increased medical need breeds work disability). For one of the three measures, one age term proved significant; for all three measures, the activity limitation terms were unrelated to the change in the employment of persons with disabilities. On balance, then, there is only weak support for the alternative hypotheses that the aging of the population and attendant growth of activity limitation are responsible for the growth in the work disability rate.

do that the year-to-year change in an industry's share of employment of workers with disabilities has a .96 correlation with the change in its overall share of employment (Table 6.7).[9] In effect, the employment prospects of workers with disabilities are almost perfectly tied to the health of the sectors in which they work. The pull of service industries notwithstanding, by and large the employment situation of persons with disabilities worsened over the last two decades as several traditional employment poles for older workers—manufacturing, construction, and extractive industries—retrenched. Thus, the push from these sectors, abetted by an explicit strategy of treating employees as parts of just-in-time inventory, is what led to the epidemic of work disability. First objectified as the leading edge of a tidal wave of aging-related medical need, then falsely maligned for choosing compensation over work, persons with disabilities instead were silently displaced from industries in decline.

A Quiet Politics Reigns

In 1981, several hundred thousand beneficiaries of SSDI had their benefits terminated upon implementation of a new regulation allowing removal from the program prior to a hearing. Ultimately, the change in the regulation proved unpopular—to understate the case—and was rescinded. The shock therapy of the early 1980s shone a light on work disability issues, bringing the plight of those thrown off the SSDI program to center stage, and in the process making the continuation of this policy untenable. In the years that followed, the United States adopted a quieter—indeed, unnoticed—strategy of using persons with disabilities to accommodate the transformation of the labor force and of again allowing the SSDI program to compensate them for this role. The compensation is inadequate. The cuts in benefit levels were not restored, so persons with disabilities, especially nonwhites, have lower incomes now than they have had for several decades. Displaced from employment opportunities a little more each year, and with progressively less access to transfer payments, the well-being of persons with disabilities is gradually being eroded. The noisy

[9]This correlation, derived from the year-to-year analysis, is slightly higher than the one cited in Table 6.4, which relied on the three selected years.

politics that followed the attack on the SSDI program in 1981 ultimately served persons with disabilities far better than did the quiet politics of the last few years, for it is often easier to fight off a frontal assault than to parry an accretion of small losses. Hidden by the subtle workings of the labor market, persons with disabilities bear a disproportionate share of the costs of industrial change, and most of us never notice.

7

Displaced by Illness, Displaced from View

Disability differs from other characteristics that subject people to discrimination. A person of color will always remain one; a woman will almost always remain one; and a person of an unpopular religion by birth will always remain one in someone else's eyes, even if not in his or her own. The Caucasian, male Protestant, particularly one living the good life in an affluent suburb, need not concern himself with the problems faced by an African-American woman or man, or even those faced by a Jewish male colleague who might want to join his country club. In many cases, he may have no regular contact with any of these people. However, he might become disabled tomorrow, and he certainly knows many people like himself who are already disabled. In acknowledging that he might face disability himself, he becomes a little more sympathetic to the plight of those with disabilities than to others experiencing discrimination.

The commonality of interests between those who already have a disability and the rest of us, who may have one in the future, protects the rights of persons with disabilities somewhat, but not completely. Disability, unlike race, sex, or religion is defined in a social context, and that social context can and does change. In the early 1980s, we decided that some disabilities, previously thought to be permanent ones, miraculously, were all of a sudden subject to medical improvement and that persons with these disabilities should have their compensation taken away until they could prove their conditions had again worsened.[1] Because disability can be defined in a social context, it was, rendering several hundred thousand persons with disabilities much worse off. And then because these relatives and friends of ours were able to call upon our compassion (and perhaps our fear that we might be in the same situation ourselves), the social context changed once more. Conditions defined as subject to improvement in 1981 are once again thought to be permanent in nature.

Subjective perceptions of persons with disabilities may waver and have wavered, but the objective conditions such people face have been worsening for two decades or more: with the exception of young women with disabilities pulled into an expanding services sector, persons with disabilities experienced a dramatic loss of employment opportunities. At a time when older workers generally have faced a slackening demand for their labor, older workers with disabilities have virtually vanished from the labor market. With less access to work, and with lower disability payments, they have seen their incomes fall as well.

From Abstract Principles to Tangible Policy

Academics have traditionally shunned disability research, viewing disability as an unglamorous arena in which to apply their brilliant expertise or as the result of an inherently simple process not worthy of their attention. Someone gets sick, stops working, and collects insurance. Abstract principle: bad things randomly

---

[1]Deborah Stone's(1984) *The Disabled State,* Edward Berkowitz's (1987) *Disabled Policy: America's Programs for the Handicapped,* and Martha Derthick's (1990) *Agency under Stress: The Social Security Administration in American Government* recount this history. Stone argues that disability compensation stands between permanently unpopular welfare and permanently popular insurance schemes in the public's eye, thus explaining why it is buffeted by the political winds in ways other programs are not. Berkowitz holds that SSDI founders because it is an incomplete expression of the desire of the American people to assist persons with disabilities get back into work and provide them with an adequate income if they cannot do so, failing to do either well and engendering much controversy in the effort. Finally, Derthick stresses the importance of the structural position of the Social Security Administration within the U.S. system of government as a cause of its inability to shield itself from periodic crises in public confidence.

happen to good people and society ought to help them. The theory works—until a demographic wave overtakes us, swamping society with increasing numbers of frail elderly and simultaneously flooding the labor market with baby boomers bent on crowding these elders out of work. Alternatively, liberal disability entitlements allow people who can work to stop doing so, to malinger. Abstract principle: bad policy allows good people, rationally equilibrating labor and leisure at the margin, to choose leisure. The theory works—until several hundred thousand SSDI recipients have been thrown off the rolls and benefit levels for the remaining beneficiaries reduced, but labor force participation rates among persons with disabilities continue to fall.

I do not mean to say that medical need never drives work disability rates. There always have been and always will be some individuals whose disabilities are too severe for any employment. However, they constitute only a small fraction of all workers, a small fraction of elderly workers, and even a small fraction of all elderly workers with chronic disease, for whom employment—or work disability—is contingent on social conditions. Twenty years ago, work demanded much more physical exertion, and yet labor force participation rates among older men with disabilities were much higher. This worsening access to the labor market occurred despite the fact that on a proportional basis, older men are no likelier to have disabilities now than in 1970, and despite the fact that older men with disabilities do not appear to have more severe impairments now than they had then. Fears about a pandemic of disease among an aging population and baby boomers crowding the labor market notwithstanding, the labor market can and did accommodate workers with disabilities when it needed to, and it accommodated record numbers of new entrants, too.

As I pointed out in Chapter 3, I do not mean to say that malingering does not occur and that benefit levels never affect employment. Malingering does occur, but we cannot predict it on the basis of any set of characteristics, including benefit levels.[2] Thus,

---

[2]In my article "The Myth of Malingering: Why Individuals Withdraw from Work in the Presence of Illness" (Yelin 1986), I show that persons with higher income replacement rates, in fact, have lower work disability rates, the opposite of what the theory that disability compensation entices persons to leave work would suggest.

it is an anecdotal truth (Worker X stopped working upon realizing that he or she could get decent SSDI benefits) and a statistical lie (among a million people just like X, benefit levels do not correlate with labor force participation rates).

Disability compensation programs were established in the abstract belief that medically severe conditions preclude work and then revised in the abstract belief that demography is rendering medical need infinite in a time of severe budgetary constraint, while entitlements make a strategy of malingering pay. However, these abstract principles conscientiously applied to policy—and they were—cause tangible pain. When medical criteria for SSDI were made more stringent, the mythical future claimants riding tomorrow's aging wave in whose name this policy was instituted were not hurt because they are still children. Several hundred thousand SSDI recipients whose chronic conditions were rendered curable with the stroke of a regulator's pen were hurt because they lost their principal source of income. The SSDI benefit reduction intended to keep the potential malingerer working pushed the person with quadriplegia into poverty.[3]

In retrospect, the notion that people would leave work to secure SSDI as part of a rational calculation seems absurd. Assume that workers know how much income they would get from work or SSDI when they decide to leave their jobs. In truth, most people have no idea what they would get from disability benefits. After waiting the mandatory six months before applying, the odds that an application will be successful are about one in four, and the expected benefits, never higher than 39 percent of average salaries, are now about a third of wages. Thus, to follow the logic, people would leave real jobs for a 25 percent chance to see their incomes fall by more than 60 percent (hence a 75 percent chance that incomes would fall even more), at a minimum lag of six months. The abstract theory of rational expectations aside, this is a bad bet. In fact, by arguing that policy alters the terms of the bet, we suggest that persons with disabilities can choose whether or not to withdraw from work, and that policy ought to make the withdrawal "option" more difficult. The growth in the work

---

[3]Wolfe and Haveman (1990) review the impact of policy changes on labor force participation of persons with disabilities; their earlier article (Haveman and Wolfe 1989) evaluated the impact on the income of these persons.

disability rate in the face of declining benefit levels belies this notion.

Social Security as the All-Punishing Nanny

In a nation always suspicious of welfare, Social Security has achieved unprecedented popularity by posing as a universalistic insurance program.[4] Pay in, get out. Conservatives attacked Social Security in the 1970s, arguing that this universality took the discipline out of markets for both labor and capital, in the former case by giving older persons as well as those with disabilities alternatives to work,[5] and in the latter by soaking up investment capital.[6] The "reforms" of the SSDI program, driven by the desire to change the disincentive to work, were designed to make disability compensation less universalistic. To do this, however, Social Security was put in the position of a stern nanny, forced to judge the veracity of medical claims of an inability to work, and then to punish the malingering by taking away their benefits. In doing so, the Social Security Administration undermined the basis of its popularity, its ability to send checks to anyone falling within its jurisdiction.[7] Although the architects of Social Security made a clear distinction among temporary disability, permanent disability, and retirement, the public does not distinguish among the parts of the entire spectrum of benefits very clearly, especially when times are as bad as they were in the early 1980s. Although the conservatives attacked all forms of Social Security, they reserved most of their venom for disability insurance because of its putative role in clearing the labor market of older workers and

[4]This is the argument made by Charles Lockhart (1989) in his: *Gaining Ground: Tailoring Social Programs to American Values,* particularly in chapter 2, "Socioeconomic Rights and American Conceptions of Distributive Justice," and by Theodore Marmor, Jerry Mashaw, and Philip Harvey (1990) in *America's Misunderstood Welfare State: Persistent Myths, Enduring Realities,* particularly on pages 47–49, which report on public attitudes toward social welfare programs.

[5]See, Gilder's (1981) *Wealth and Poverty* and Charles Murray's (1984) *Losing Ground.*

[6]Feldstein (1974), for example, in his article, "Social Security and Private Capital Accumulation: International Evidence in an Extended Life-Cycle Model," is the foremost proponent of this view.

[7]See Derthick 1990, especially 33–46.

because it paid relatively high benefits.[8] For years, Social Security had been sold on the basis of its universality, covering all risks for all persons of all ages. The public was not about to forget this when they needed to draw upon it.

Taking the Nanny out of Disability Policy

The distinction among public insurance programs is in fact arbitrary. In the United States, long-term care takes its definition from Medicare acute care hospitalization rules rather than from the sense that certain pathologies ought be taken care of in one sort of institution, others in another sort.[9] Likewise, short-term disability insurance—usually issued on behalf of the firm for its employees or on behalf of the state for its residents—covers work loss prior to the six month waiting period established by the SSDI program as a way of keeping people from leaving work to get benefits, in effect filling a hole in the social insurance continuum purposefully left open by SSDI.[10] Finally, many countries tacitly accept that disability insurance programs act as a form of early retirement program, seeing this set of expenditures as a politically expeditious way of clearing the labor market when the demand for labor becomes slack.[11] Indeed, retirement itself is a relatively new phenomenon, and public and even private pension programs are even newer.[12] Retirement at age 55 (when many private pensions kick in), at age 62 (to collect Social Security at the earliest age allowable), at age 65 (to collect full Social Security benefits at the earliest age currently allowed), or at age 67 (to collect full Social Security benefits at the earliest age allowed my generation)[13] reflects actuarial estimates of the health of the population first made more than fifty years ago or actuarial estimates of the health

[8]Berkowitz (1987, especially 111–130), recounts the way arguments about the effect of the replacement rate on the incentive to work shaped all discussion of the SSDI program.

[9]See "Program Description" in U.S. Department of Health and Human Services (1990b, especially 54, 56–58, and 63–64).

[10]See Berkowitz 1987, especially 61–64.

[11]See Burkhauser and Hirvonen 1989; and Berkowitz 1989.

[12]See Graebner (1980) for a history of retirement and retirement policy.

[13]See U.S. Department of Health and Human Services (1990b, 23–32) for a description of when retirement may take place under the Social Security program; see Graebner (1980) for how these rules were established.

of the Social Security trust fund made more recently, not a con-
sensual decision about how much leisure time the typical person
should enjoy, let alone how tight the labor market ought to be.

The labor force participation rate, and hence the proportion of
the population drawing income from wages and salaries versus
any form of public insurance, also is not set in stone, nor does it
have to be determined completely by market forces. High labor
force participation rates have obvious benefits, giving more people the sense of self-worth that comes from work and spreading
the risk of unemployment across family members, but they also
have their costs, reducing wages of all workers, increasing day
care expenses, taxing family time, and so on. Other nations, including some apparently as successful, if not more so, than the
United States, take another route, putting fewer people to work
and paying higher social wages to those out of the labor force.[14] In
Germany, for example, only 51.9 percent of the working-age population are in the labor force. However, the wages earned by many
fewer workers yield approximately equal per capita incomes for
the population, meaning that the proportion of wages re-
distributed as social insurance is much higher.[15] The real, total
value of the wages generated in work matters, but the distribution
of that product can take many forms.[16]

Prior to the early 1980s, the United States had an implicit policy
of allowing SSDI to accommodate slack markets for labor by
providing a soft landing for older workers with disabilities. The
growth of the SSDI program in the 1970s brought that policy into
question. However, at its peak, SSDI took only about 1 percent of
the GNP. While malingering is lamentable in theory (who among
us can muster any sympathy for the harried clerk claiming
stress?), in practice this was a small price to pay to compensate
those cleared from the labor market, especially given that at least
as many persons with disabilities experienced discrimination in
hiring and firing as purposefully took the disability compensation

[14]See U.S. Department of Labor (1990b, 99) for data on employment-to-
population ratios. The U.S. employment-to-population ratio of 63.0 percent is
slightly higher than Japan's (60.8 percent), but much higher than Germany's
(51.9 percent), France's (50.2 percent), and Italy's (43.4 percent).

[15]See U.S. Bureau of the Census 1990, 840–841.

[16]This is the viewpoint expressed by Frank Levy and Richard Murnane
(1991) in a recent news article.

route, and few of those who would easily qualify for benefits ever applied.

SSDI plays a critical role in perpetuating the myth that the market can and should determine who works and who does not, allowing a reasonably large fraction of the older working-age population an out when they get displaced, while providing no other age group such recourse. Many, if not most, would work if there were jobs for them; the situation little more than two decades ago attests to this. The cutbacks in the SSDI program were designed explicitly to close the safety valve, reserving the program only for those with the most serious physical impairments. The politics of the SSDI program being what they are, most of the severe cutbacks were rescinded. Having succeeded in reducing the share of GNP going to SSDI recipients 50 percent by cutting the real value of benefits and including fewer dependents as beneficiaries, the "reforms" took a real toll on persons with disabilities. Nevertheless, the basic architecture of the program remains intact. With the number of disabled-worker beneficiaries again growing, SSDI continues to serve as a safety valve, allowing policymakers to postpone coming up with a more explicit way of allocating people to jobs and allocating income to wages, pensions, and social insurance.

There are as many ways to make these allocations as there are advanced industrial nations. Some nations allow earlier retirement, shorter work weeks, more vacation, extended unemployment benefits, compensation for displacement from declining industries, and, yes, even more liberal disability criteria.[17] The United States has changed the allocation, but not by explicit criteria. Compared to the 1960s, greater proportions of the adult population work, but fewer older workers do. Those who are in jobs receive lower wages, work fewer hours, and have less security. Some, but not all, of the older workers who have left the labor force early are entitled to SSDI. Tacitly accepting the notion that workers with disabilities are less able to work, or merely using illness as the most legitimate way to clear the labor market, the United States has adopted a public policy of using work

[17]See Haanes-Olsen (1989) for a description of how other nations allocate jobs and incomes within their populations.

disability in general and SSDI in particular to accommodate the transformation of the labor force. The almost perfect correlation between industry-specific change in employment and change in employment among persons with disabilities attests to this.

Social expenditures, especially federal social expenditures, have fallen dramatically in the last decade or so.[18] Given this political climate, it would be folly to suggest major new expenditures, let alone a more explicit way of allocating work and incomes. However, one can make a good argument that persons with disabilities have not been adequately compensated for performing a very useful function. Forced to experience a disproportionate amount of retrenchment at work, they have seen SSDI, their principal source of income, fall by half. More important, at a time when the physical basis of work is eroding, the implicit strategy of accommodating retrenchment through workers with disabilities perpetuates the notion that such persons are any less able to continue working than those allowed to maintain their jobs, in effect, paying them to acquiesce in discrimination against them.

There would appear to be more rational ways to compensate people for being out of the labor force than disability status. Providing more education to young adults might actually pay a return on the expenditure while accomplishing the same goal. Allowing mid-career training leaves, or timeoff to care for children and parents, could do so as well. On the other hand, if we determine that we truly want to aid the transition from an old to a young work force, I would favor melding SSDI and Social Security retirement expenditures for workers over 50.[19] Workers could gradually phase out work time, substituting an increasing portion of early retirement benefits for forgone wages, or they could stop working altogether, in either case reducing the amount of the Social Security benefits they will get after age 65, just as they do now when retiring between ages 62 and 65. This program

[18]Bixby (1991) shows that the percentage of GNP spent on social welfare expenditures in 1991 had fallen more than 5 percent since peaking in 1976; the portion of the federal budget going to social welfare expenditures fell about 11 percent in the same period.

[19]Haanes-Olsen (1989, 23) describes programs in Sweden, Denmark, Finland, and France that allow melding of wages with a partial payment from the public retirement funds.

could be designed to have a neutral effect on each individual's lifetime Social Security benefits; alternatively, it could be designed so that the individual actually took less over his or her lifetime in exchange for drawing upon benefits prior to age 62, in effect, creating an incentive to stay in the labor force. The decrease in the lifetime Social Security benefit would always be greater for those who do not work at all than for those working part-time. Likewise, movement from nonwork to part-time work and from part-time to full-time employment would allow one to buy back increasing proportions of the benefits lost by drawing upon Social Security prior to age 62. Those who could not find work but wanted to stay employed would be supported to the federal poverty level to do public service jobs and could continue to build up Social Security credits, albeit at a level consistent with these low wages.

Given the discrimination against persons with disabilities, such workers would be more likely to take advantage of this program than those without disabilities. However, technically, the program would be universalistic, open to all workers, taking the Social Security Administration out of its role as a SSDI nanny. Designed to be neutral with respect to the fiscal health of Social Security, while allowing each person access to his or her benefits when he or she deems it necessary, the program would encourage those able to sustain employment to stay in the labor force by allowing the individual flexible options to increase future income by working more hours without risking the loss of all current benefits, as is now the case with the SSDI program. Indeed, one of the principal ironies of the U.S. social welfare system is that while espousing work, we make an attempt to return to employment risky. The architecture of the SSDI program itself is not alone in this bias. An individual who ventures into the labor market will eventually forfeit either the Medicare benefits that accompany SSDI payments or the Medicaid benefits that come with SSI or AFDC. Indeed, there is good evidence that basing health insurance on employment keeps workers from changing jobs even when they want to switch and their employers want them to leave because potential new jobs do not include health insurance or exclude preexisting conditions.[20]

[20]See Uchitelle 1991c; and Sing 1990.

Public Policy in the Era of the Rubber Band

I have shown that persons with disabilities are the wrong kind of leading edge, being the first fired from industries shedding workers and the last hired in ascending ones. Older workers generally are vanishing from the labor market, but older workers with disabilities are vanishing faster than are those without them. Public policy toward disability is not concerned with these trends. To the extent policy initiatives reflect collective angst, we worry about work disability because we fear that a pandemic of aging-related medical need will swamp Medicare, or we worry about the impact of disability benefits on the incentive to work, or we worry about the absolute cost of disability benefit programs. Thus, public policy toward disability becomes a sideshow for other concerns about the fiscal health of the economy in general and the federal government in particular.

Work disability can be displaced from public view by the arbitrary decision to reduce benefit levels, but this has no effect whatsoever on the real problem of declining labor force participation among persons with disabilities. The fiscal health of the SSDI trust fund ebbs and flows, but the employment situation of persons with disabilities just gets worse. Among all older workers with disabilities, in fact, labor force participation rates declined by 27 percent in just two decades—and older nonwhite men with disabilities saw their labor force participation rates fall by close to half.

The disproportionate increase in work disability rates among minority men suggests that this problem is tied to more general labor market trends. As noted in Chapter 4, the sociologist William Julius Wilson (1987) argues in a highly publicized and controversial book that the decline of inner-city industry rather than discrimination per se accounts for the growing problem of ghetto unemployment.[21] To my mind, it is hard to separate the denuding of inner-city industry from discrimination, since conscious decisions in both the public and private spheres have abetted this process. Nevertheless, like Wilson, I have shown that industrial change affects well-being, in this case by propelling

[21]See Wilson's (1987) *The Truly Disadvantaged: The Inner City, The Underclass, and Public Policy,* especially chapter 6, "The Limited Visions of Race Relations and the War on Poverty."

older workers with disabilities out of industries undergoing retrenchment. That being so, disability policy cannot be separated from industrial policy.

Some argue that we should take a hands-off approach to industrial transformation, that the invisible hand will necessarily lead us to the best mix of industries. However, to accede to this line of reasoning would condemn persons with disabilities to even higher rates of work loss since, being disproportionately old, they are also disproportionately represented in manufacturing industries systematically shedding workers. Moreover, two decades during which the standard of living has been falling suggest that inattention to the well-being of manufacturing will not, willy nilly, allow us to continue as a prosperous nation. Persons with disabilities, especially nonwhite ones, pay a steeper price for industrial transformation, but we are all paying.

What Goes Down May Go Up, but How Long from Now?

The rubber band proved much more elastic in shedding older persons with disabilities from the labor force than in bringing young ones in. Nevertheless, the tightening demand for labor in service industry did bring jobs to thousands of workers with disabilities, particularly during the 1980s. Some might claim that after the post-industrial transformation has run its course, persons with disabilities will have been reintegrated into the labor force. However, the service boom that helped some persons with disabilities find jobs during the 1980s would appear to be over. Employment levels stopped growing in this sector even before the 1990-1992 recession began, and by early 1992 all but medical industries in the service sector were laying off workers.[22] More important, the laissez-faire strategy condemns persons with disabilities to the end of the labor market queue even though they have the physical capacity to do most of the work in the current economy. And it suggests that nothing can be done in the short term to keep them in the labor force.

Nothing could be further from the truth. Physical impairment

[22]See U.S. Department of Labor 1991c, 70. See also Nasar 1991b; and Uchitelle 1991b.

rarely is the main reason the person with a disability does not keep working anymore. Most service work makes no physical demands. And much "physical work" now involves nothing more strenuous than monitoring a digitalized version of a physical process on a computer screen, frequently at some remove from where the work is being done. Instead, persons with disabilities face a disjuncture between the rhythms of chronic disease and the rhythms of work. Industrial-strength working conditions make no sense for most of the work in the contemporary economy, and they create artificial impediments for persons with disabilities. Often, these people can fulfill all the tangible requirements of the job, but are forced to stop working because they cannot meet an arbitrary rule that work be performed at a standard pace and during standard hours of operation. Many times employers will use the disjuncture between chronic disease and work rules to legitimate disproportionate layoffs among persons with disabilities ("You can't be here for eight consecutive hours; you can't keep this job").

Thus, in the long term, the plight of persons with disabilities is tied to more general trends in the economy, but much can be done in the short term to keep these persons employed by making the fit between the rhythms of illness and the rhythms of work more rational. Ironically, the decline of the manufacturing sector occurred, at least in part, because industrial-strength working conditions are no longer successful. In that sense, what was bad for General Motors was bad for all of us, but it was devastating for persons with disabilities, particularly older and nonwhite ones.

A Safe Harbor, Not a Sheltered Cove

Public policy for persons with disabilities tilts toward compensation, and to the extent it covers employment, it does so by emphasizing sheltered employment. This history of public programs for persons with disabilities is paradoxical. In general, the American public wants social welfare expenditures that help people (some would say force them) to enter the labor market. There is good evidence that such expenditures on behalf of most, if not all, persons with disabilities are ultimately costless insofar as an investment in rehabilitation now gets paid off in taxes later, and yet almost all of our energies go into disability compensation.

Furthermore, much of our rehabilitation aims low: to place persons with disabilities in "sheltered" employment paying far less than prevailing wages and in noncompetitive sectors of the economy.

I do not want to dismiss all such efforts. Many persons have disabilities so severe that they will never be able to obtain competitive employment. Others need a bridge to jobs in the competitive sectors. However, all too often people are referred to sheltered employment on the basis of false stereotypes about their true functional capacity, or out of fear that the person so referred might face discrimination based on physical appearance as much as anything else, or simply so that the agency making the referral can claim a successful case closure.

Moreover, sheltered employment fails when it is made the centerpiece of public policy efforts. It fails because it is dependent upon public sector support, which is rarely forthcoming during bad times, when need is greatest. More important, almost by definition, sheltered employment operates only in noncompetitive markets, meaning consignment to the declining sectors of the economy and/or those with a permanently low-wage structure. SSDI "pays" more than many of these jobs, and in some situations, SSI does so as well.

I also do not mean to suggest that rehabilitation never aims high, to place individuals in competitive employment. Pushed by the disability rights movement, particularly the independent living centers, rehabilitation professionals became strong advocates for mainstreaming persons with disabilities into competitive employment. However, such persons have received no help from policymakers, perhaps because more than a decade of antigovernment fervor paralyzed us all into believing that nothing creative could be done on the policy front, or that if it could be done, it would be too expensive. Medical care, in particular, stands indicted on this score. Medical care can do wonders for the individual—who can scoff at the impact of the joint replacement or kidney transplant on the overall quality of life? However, it can rarely be justified solely on the basis of its effect on return to work. Total joint replacement surgery, for example, has only a minimal effect on the labor force participation rates of those receiving this procedure.[23]

[23]See, for example, Nevitt et al. 1984; and Liang et al. 1986.

Thus, the bulk of public policy related to the employment of persons with disabilities takes a passive stance, compensating the individual for staying out of work, and much of the remainder takes an expensive one, paying for individual-level medical and (less frequently) rehabilitation services.

The research described in this book demonstrates that work disability is inherently contextual, meaning that work disability occurs because of the interaction of characteristics of the individual and characteristics of the environment, including the economic environment. In turn, public policy can intervene at the level of the individual through medical and rehabilitation services or by promoting a better fit between the individual and the environment. Systematic intervention for the individual through medical and rehabilitation services has had limited success and has been very expensive. I believe public policy can be much more effective in improving the employment situation of persons with disabilities by intervening on the other side of the template, by fostering working conditions conducive to the maintenance of work and by focusing employment efforts on those industries with the potential to expand their work forces. In effect, I am arguing for a safe harbors policy, in which public policy systematically describes the industries and workplaces that can and do hire persons with disabilities, and assists them in doing so, while fighting discrimination against such persons in firms not giving them their proportionate share of work.

Some employers have taken it upon themselves to initiate a nascent version of a safe harbors policy. Called disability management, the policy is intended to reduce disability compensation premiums by preventive measures, including putting persons with disabilities into work environments in which they can thrive.[24] However, the actuarial goal of reducing premiums may be achieved without increasing the number of persons with disabilities actually employed—perhaps by discriminating against them in hiring in the first place, perhaps by changing the terms under which claimants may become entitled to benefits. Thus, just as the problems in the SSDI program were solved without increasing the proportion of persons with disabilities in the labor force, disability management will not in of itself ensure safe employment harbors.

[24]See Watson 1990.

The regulations to implement the Americans with Disabilities Act[25] provide guidance in creating a true safe harbors policy for persons with disabilities. Under this act, individuals cannot be denied access to a job if they can perform its "essential function," those tasks that define the job (for example, filing and typing for a secretary, but not fetching coffee). Employers must provide assistance and modifications to the work environment when necessary to ensure that a person can perform a job's essential functions, unless doing so would place an undue burden on the firm, meaning that it would have to cease operations. Even if the provision of assistance and modifications would place an undue burden on the firm, the individuals must still have access to the job if they are willing to pay for these themselves.

Earlier, I provided ample evidence that persons with disabilities experienced disproportionately small amounts of hiring in ascending industries and disproportionately large layoffs from declining ones, albeit from data collected for another purpose and distributed years later. The Americans with Disabilities Act vests individuals with the responsibility to prove that they were denied access to jobs for which they could do the essential functions by taking their allegations before the Equal Employment Opportunity Commission (EEOC). However, on the basis of the experience with the Rehabilitation Act of 1973 and civil rights legislation affecting women and minorities, only a fraction of those who might successfully bring such claims can be expected to do so.[26] The cost of pursuing discrimination cases to the EEOC accounts for this, but only in part. A more important reason is that there are no timely statistics available with which to prove that the failure to get a job represents a disproportionate impact, and none to establish that persons like the individual pursuing the case can and do perform the essential functions of similar jobs. Thus, we need to establish a faster and more reliable way of assessing the employment dynamics among persons with disabilities.

Each month the government collects employment statistics as part of the Bureau of Labor Statistics' *Current Population Survey* (CPS). These data make page one of most newspapers, publicizing the employment situation of women, minorities, and youth. In

---

[25]Equal Employment Opportunity Commission 1991.
[26]See Yelin 1991.

contrast, the CPS currently collects information about the labor force participation of persons with disabilities only once a year, in its March Supplement. The cumulative results have been published only twice in the last decade, and then only in the form of government statistical reports, so the findings have been relegated to an academic audience.[27] The addition of questions about disability status to the monthly CPS would assist persons with disabilities in demonstrating that they experience disproportionate impacts of labor market dynamics and would show employers that such persons function well in similar work situations. The disability screen would add less than a minute to the monthly CPS interview. Aside from helping to establish discrimination, the data from the CPS would also assist in targeting referrals of persons with disabilities to growing sectors of the economy, while avoiding sending them to sectors in decline.

Clearly, much of the discrimination against persons with disabilities is based on the fear, unfounded, that accommodating their needs in the workplace will be expensive. This fear stems from the mistaken notions that most persons with disabilities have severe impairments, that the physical requirements of jobs and the physical structure of the workplace are the major impediment to employment, and that accommodating these physical needs requires huge expenditures of money. The reality is that the great majority of persons with disabilities have subtle impairments that emerge gradually from the traditional chronic diseases of aging,[28] that they leave work because fitting the time requirements of jobs together with the rhythms of illness is difficult,[29] and that they require physical accommodations costing less than several hundred dollars.[30] A single step is as much an impediment to employment as an entire flight of stairs, and a much more common one at that.

Thus, employers fear that lengthy regulations necessarily will follow any attempt to intervene on the workplace side of the ledger, and that expensive alterations in the physical environment and in work rules also will ensue. And policymakers fear that

[27]See U.S. Bureau of the Census 1983a, 1989b.
[28]See LaPlante 1988.
[29]See, for example, Yelin, Henke, and Epstein 1987; Yelin et al. 1991.
[30]See Collignon 1986.

government will have to expend huge sums of money to regulate the work environment of a million firms, and will engender only a bitter backlash for its efforts.

Paralyzed by these fears, and sustained by antigovernment sentiment, we have avoided many of the traditional policy tools available to assist in the hiring of persons of disabilities even when we have good evidence that these tools are inexpensive. We know that strong architectural standards impose relatively small costs on employers and virtually none on government, and that they improve the employability of persons with disabilities. Likewise, we know that any direct cash assistance government provides to help workplaces modify their physical environment will more than come back in tax revenues, albeit at a lag. We know, too, that flexible work rules reduce the work disability rate, but we have devised neither a mechanism to convince employers of this nor one to assist in implementing such rules. Perhaps something like an agricultural extension service for working conditions is in order, in which government agents would travel to employers, teaching them how to institute a more flexible set of work rules. However, the erosion of the labor unions and the declining strength of labor force regulatory agencies take away all the pressure on recalcitrant employers to negotiate the kind of working conditions that would allow more persons with disabilities to get and stay employed. Ironically, the unionized work force has lower work disability rates.[31] The fear of loosening control over work rules and the fear of unions make many employers their own worst enemy.

Thus, there is much we could do to create safe harbors in employment for persons with disabilities, and at little cost, including collecting information on their labor force participation, both to assist in making a case for discrimination and to help target referrals; using tax incentives to assist in making modifications and induce additional hiring; and helping negotiate work rules conducive to maintenance of jobs. There is much in disability policy that does work, but little that can work given the current political climate.

Even so, the most creative disability policies at the level of the individual workplace will have limited success until we increase

[31]See Yelin 1986.

the demand for labor, particularly in the manufacturing sector, which shed so many older workers with disabilities over the last decade or so. Those holding that medical need and disability claims can expand infinitely were correct, but their reasoning was wrong. Medical need and disability claims will only express themselves in a context, that context being the general decline of employment opportunities. Some analysts shamelessly blamed older workers for their health status; others, for their putative malingering. The decline of manufacturing industries and the decline of manufacturing employment are more troubling phenomena because, unlike the cost crisis in medicine or in SSDI, they cannot be dealt with by actions as simple as cutting benefit levels.

The "essential functions" clause of the Americans with Disabilities Act, progressively intentioned, may retard the long-term employability of persons with disabilities precisely because it models work in a way more consistent with a more primitive form of industrialism. Workplaces organized on the principles of continuous improvement flatten hierarchies, placing a greater number of tasks within each job, in turn making it much harder to define the essential functions of the job. The job easily reduced to an essential function, in contrast, may meet the letter of the act, while providing no long-term security. The safest harbor for the person with disabilities is a workplace that can succeed, as the unfortunate experience of those employed in the manufacturing sector over the last two decades proves.

Displaced by Illness, Displaced from View

Joseph Schumpeter coined the oxymoronic term *creative destruction* to show that prosperity increases when societies substitute new industries with the potential for growth in profits for older ones whose potential is spent. Ever since the Enclosure Acts, some people have been displaced when activities generating higher incomes for the society as a whole replace old ones. Historically, this process has hurt those people in industries being overtaken. In the long run, many displaced from one set of activities have been reintegrated into others, perhaps even experiencing a rise in their own standard of living along the way. Over the last two decades, the destructive part has been occurring, as millions of workers have been displaced from declining industries, but the creative part has not run its course, so the overall standard of living has been stagnant.[32]

I have tried to show that persons with disabilities have suffered from this dynamic. The noisy politics surrounding the SSDI program in the early 1980s brought their situation to the public's attention, evoking the special bond that the public has with the problems of persons with disabilities. As a result, the government rescinded some of the cutbacks, taking the work disability issue off center stage for the remainder of the decade. The public's perception that the crisis in work disability is over notwithstanding, persons with disabilities have even less access to the labor market than they did ten years ago. First displaced by illness from industries undergoing transformation, persons with disabilities have since been displaced from view.

---

[32]See Levy and Murnane (1991) for the evidence that real wages have stagnated.

References

Aaron, H., and G. Burtless. 1984. *Retirement and Economic Behavior.* Washington, D.C.: Brookings Institution.

Aaron, H., and W. Schwartz. 1984. *The Painful Prescription: Rationing Hospital Care.* Washington, D.C.: Brookings Institution.

Achenbaum, W. 1986. *Social Security: Visions and Revisions.* New York: Cambridge University Press.

Argyris, C. 1982. *Reasoning, Learning, and Action: Individual and Organizational.* San Francisco: Jossey-Bass.

Atchley, R. 1982. Retirement as a Social Institution. *Annual Review of Sociology* 8:263–287.

Ball, R. 1978. *Social Security: Today and Tomorrow.* New York: Columbia University Press.

Bell, D. 1973. *The Coming of Post-Industrial Society: A Venture in Social Forecasting.* New York: Basic Books.

Belous, R. 1989. *The Contingent Economy: The Growth of the Temporary, Part-Time, and Subcontracted Workforce.* Washington, D.C.: National Planning Association.

Berkowitz, E. 1987. *Disabled Policy: America's Programs for the Handicapped.* New York: Cambridge University Press.

———. 1989. Domestic Politics and International Expertise in the History of American Disability Policy. *Milbank Quarterly* 67 (supp. 2, part 1): 195–227.

Berkowitz, M., W. Johnson, and E. Murphy. 1976. *Public Policy Toward Disability.* New York: Praeger.

Best, M. 1990. *The New Competition: Institutions of Industrial Restructuring.* Cambridge: Harvard University Press.

Better, S., P. Fine, D. Simison, et al. 1979. Disability Benefits as Disincentives to Rehabilitation. *Milbank Memorial Fund Quarterly: Health and Society* 57(3): 412–427.

Birren, J., P. Robinson, and J. Livingston, eds. 1981. *Age, Health, and Employment.* Englewood Cliffs, N.J.: Prentice-Hall.

Bixby, A. 1991. Public Social Welfare Expenditures, Fiscal Year 1988. *Social Security Bulletin* 54(5): 2–16.

Blackburn, M., D. Bloom, and R. Freeman. 1990. The Declining Economic Position of Less Skilled American Men. In *A Future of Lousy Jobs: The Changing Structure of U.S. Wages,* edited by G. Burtless. Washington, D.C.: Brookings Institution.

———. 1991. An Era of Falling Earnings and Rising Inequality? *Brookings Review* 9(1): 38–43.

Blanc, P. and E. Yelin. 1991. Asthma Severity as a Predictor of Work Disability among Persons with Asthma. *American Review of Respiratory Disease* 143:A269.

Blank, R. and A. Blinder. 1986. Macroeconomics, Income Distribution, and Poverty. In *Fighting Poverty: What Works and What Doesn't,* edited by S. Danziger and D. Weinberg. Cambridge: Harvard University Press.

Blank, R. 1990. Are Part-Time Jobs Bad Jobs? In *A Future of Lousy Jobs: The Changing Structure of U.S. Wages,* edited by G. Burtless. Washington, D.C.: Brookings Institution.

Block, F. 1987. Rethinking the Political Economy of the Welfare State. In *The Mean Season: The Attack on the Welfare State,* edited by F. Block, R. Cloward, B. Ehrenreich, and F. Piven. New York: Pantheon.

———. 1990. *Postindustrial Possibilities: A Critique of Economic Discourse.* Berkeley: University of California Press.

Bluestone, B. 1990. The Impact of Schooling and Industrial Restructuring on Recent Trends in Wage Inequality in the United States. *American Economic Review* 80(2): 303–307.

Bluestone, B. and B. Harrison. 1982. *The Deindustrialization of America: Plant Closings, Community Abandonment, and the Dismantling of Basic Industry.* New York: Basic Books.

———. 1986. *The Great American Jobs Machine: The Proliferation of Low Wage Employment in the U.S. Economy.* Report to the Joint Economic Committee, U.S. Congress.

Boskin, M. and M. Hurd. 1984. The Effect of Social Security on Retirement in the Early 1970's. *Quarterly Journal of Economics* 99: 767–790.

Braverman, H. 1974. *Labor and Monopoly Capital: The Degradation of Work in the Twentieth Century.* New York: Monthly Review Press.

Buitelaar, W., ed. 1988. *Technology and Work: Labour Studies in England, Germany, and the Netherlands.* London: Gower Publishing.

Burawoy, M. 1979. *Manufacturing Consent: Changes in the Labor Process under Monopoly Capitalism.* Chicago: University of Chicago Press.

Burke, T. and J. Morton. 1990. How Firm Size and Industry Affect Employee Benefits. *Monthly Labor Review* 113(12): 35–43.

Burkhauser, R. and R. Haveman. 1982. *Disability and Work: The Eco-*

nomics of American Policy. Baltimore: Johns Hopkins University Press.

Burkhauser, R. and P. Hirvonen. 1989. United States Disability Policy in a Time of Economic Crisis: A Comparison with Sweden and the Federal Republic of Germany. *Milbank Quarterly* 67 (supp. 2, part 1), 166–194.

Burtless, G. and R. Moffitt. 1984. Effect of Social Security Benefits on Labor Supply. In *Retirement and Economic Behavior,* edited by H. Aaron and G. Burtless. Washington, D.C.: Brookings Institution.

Burtless, G. 1987. Inequality in America: Where Do We Stand? *Brookings Review* 5(3): 9–16.

Buss, T. and F. Redburn. 1988. *Hidden Unemployment: Discouraged Workers and Public Policy.* New York: Praeger.

Cain, G. 1976. The Challenge of Segmented Labor Market Theories to Orthodox Theory: A Survey. *Journal of Economic Literature* 14(4): 1215–1257.

Callahan, D. 1990. *What Kind of Life: The Limits of Medical Progress.* New York: Simon and Schuster.

Carey, M. and K. Hazelbaker. 1986. Employment Growth in the Temporary Help Industry. *Monthly Labor Review* 109(4): 37–44.

Chandler, A. 1977. *The Visible Hand: The Managerial Revolution in American Business.* Cambridge, Mass.: Belknap Press.

———. 1990. *Scale and Scope: The Dynamics of Industrial Capitalism.* Cambridge, Mass.: Belknap Press.

Chapman, S., M. LaPlante, and G. Wilensky. 1986. Life Expectancy and Health Status of the Aged. *Social Security Bulletin* 49(10): 24–48.

Chinui, J., K. Murphy, and B. Pierce. 1989. Wage Inequality and the Rise in the Returns to Skill. Paper presented at the meeting of the Allied Social Science Association, December.

Chirikos, T. 1986. Accounting for the Historical Rise in Work Disability Prevalence. *Milbank Quarterly* 64(2): 271–301.

Chirikos, T. and G. Nestel. 1984. Economic Determinants and Consequences of Self-Reported Work Disability. *Journal of Health Economics* 3:117–136.

Clark, R. and J. Spengler. 1978. Changing Demography and Dependency Costs: The Implications of Future Dependency Ratios and Their Composition. In *Aging and Income: Programs and Prospects for the Elderly,* edited by B. Herzog. New York: Human Sciences Press.

Coale, A. 1964. How A Population Ages or Grows Younger. In *Population: The Vital Revolution,* edited by Ronald Freedman. New York: Anchor.

Cohen, S. and J. Zysman. 1987. *Manufacturing Matters: The Myth of the Post-Industrial Economy.* New York: Basic Books.

Cole, R. 1979. *Work, Mobility, and Participation: A Comparative Study of American and Japanese Industry.* Berkeley: University of California Press.

Collignon, F. 1986. The Role of Reasonable Accommodation in Employing Disabled Persons in Private Industry. In *Disability and the Labor Market,* edited by M. Berkowitz and M. Hill. Ithaca, N.Y.: ILR Press.

Colvez, A. and M. Blanchet. 1981. Disability Trends in the United States Population, 1966–1976. *American Journal of Public Health* 71(5): 464–471.

Commonwealth Fund. 1990. *Over 50, Ready and Able to Work.* New York: Commonwealth Fund.

————. 1991. *New Findings Show Why Employing Workers Over 50 Makes Good Financial Sense for Companies.* New York: Commonwealth Fund.

Cooper, C. 1988. White Collar Pay in Nonservice Industries, March 1988. *Monthly Labor Review* 111(10): 39–47.

Cornfield, D., ed. 1987. *Workers, Managers, and Technological Change: Emerging Patterns of Labor Relations.* New York: Plenum.

Crimmins, E. and M. Pramaggione. 1988. Changing Health of the Older Working Age Population and Retirement Patterns over Time. In *Issues in Contemporary Retirement,* edited by R. Ricardo-Campbell and E. Lazear. Stanford, Calif.: Hoover Institution Press.

Cyert, R. and C. Mowery, eds. 1988. *The Impact of Technological Change on Employment and Economic Growth.* Cambridge, Mass.: Ballinger Press.

Daniels, N. 1988. *Am I My Parents' Keeper? An Essay on Justice Between the Young and Old.* New York: Oxford University Press.

Danziger, S. and R. Plotnick. 1982. The War on Income Poverty: Achievements and Failures. In *Welfare Reform in America,* edited by P. Sommers. Hingham, Mass.: Kluwer-Nijhoff Publishing.

Danziger, S. and P. Gottschalk. 1986. Work, Poverty, and the Working Poor: A Multifaceted Problem. *Monthly Labor Review* 109(9): 17–21.

Denison, E. 1974. *Accounting for U.S. Economic Growth, 1929–1969.* Washington, D.C.: Brookings Institution.

Derthick, M. 1979. *Policymaking for Social Security.* Washington, D.C.: Brookings Institution.

————. 1990. *Agency under Stress: The Social Security Administration in American Government.* Washington, D.C.: Brookings Institution.

Dertouzos, M., R. Lester, R. Solow, and the MIT Commission on Industrial Productivity. 1989. *Made in America: Regaining the Productive Edge.* Cambridge: MIT Press.

Easterlin, R. [1980] 1987. *Birth and Fortune: The Impact of Numbers on Personal Welfare.* Chicago: University of Chicago Press.

Edwards, R. 1979. *Contested Terrain: The Transformation of the Workplace in the 20th Century.* New York: Basic Books.

Ellwood, D. 1986. The Spatial Mismatch Hypothesis: Are There Teenage Jobs Missing in the Ghetto? In *The Black Youth Employment Crisis,* edited by R. Freeman and H. Holzer. Chicago: University of Chicago Press.

———. 1988. *Poor Support: Poverty in the American Family.* New York: Basic Books.

Equal Employment Opportunity Commission. 1991. Equal Employment Opportunity of Individuals with Disabilities (final rule). 29 CFR Part 1630. *Federal Register,* July 26, 35726–35756.

Erickson, K. 1986. On Work and Alienation. *American Sociological Review* 51(February): 1–8.

Evans, S. and B. Nelson. 1989. *Wage Justice: Comparable Worth and the Paradox of Technocratic Reform.* Chicago: University of Chicago Press.

Feldstein, M. 1974. Social Security and Private Capital Accumulation: International Evidence in an Extended Life-Cycle Model. Harvard Institute of Economic Research Discussion Paper. Unpublished.

Flaim, P. and E. Sehgal. 1985. *Displaced Workers, 1979–1983.* U.S. Department of Labor Bulletin 2240.

Foner, A. and K. Schwab. 1983. Work and Retirement in a Changing Society. In *Aging in Society: Selected Reviews of Recent Research,* edited by M. Riley, B. Hess, and K. Bond. Hillsdale, N.J.: Lawrence Erlbaum Associates.

Fox, A. 1984. Income Changes at and after Social Security Benefit Receipt: Evidence from the Retirement History Study. *Social Security Bulletin* 47(9): 3 23.

Fox, D. and J. Stone. 1980. Black Lung: Miners' Militancy and Medical Uncertainty, 1968–1972. *Bulletin of the History of Medicine* 54: 43–63.

Fox, D. and D. Willis. 1989. Introduction to Disability Policy: Restoring Socioeconomic Independence. *Milbank Quarterly* 67 (supp. 2, part 1): 1–13.

Franke, R. 1979. The Hawthorne Experiments: Re-view. *American Sociological Review* 44:861–867.

———. 1980. Worker Productivity at Hawthorne. *American Sociological Review* 45:1006–1027.

Franke, R. and J. Kaul. 1978. The Hawthorne Experiments: First Statistical Interpretation. *American Sociological Review* 43:623–643.

Fries J. 1980. Aging, Natural Death and the Compression of Morbidity. *New England Journal of Medicine* 303: 130–135.

———. 1988. Aging, Illness, and Health Policy: Implications of the Compression of Morbidity. *Perspectives in Biology and Medicine* 31(3): 407–423.

———. 1989. Compression of Morbidity: Near or Far. *Milbank Quarterly* 67(2): 208–232.

Gartner, A. and F. Riessman. 1974. *The Service Society and the Consumer Vanguard.* New York: Harper and Row.

Gilder, G. 1981. *Wealth and Poverty.* New York: Basic Books.

Gohmann, S. 1990. Retirement Differences Among the Respondents to the Retirement History Survey. *Journal of Gerontology* 45(3): S120–127.

Graebner, W. 1980. *A History of Retirement: The Meaning and Function of an American Institution, 1885–1978.* New Haven: Yale University Press.

Greenwald, H., S. Dirks, E. Borgatta, M. McCorkle, M. Nevitt, E. Yelin. 1989. Work Disability among Cancer Patients. *Social Science and Medicine* 29(11): 1253–1259.

Gruenberg, E. 1977. The Failure of Success. *Milbank Memorial Fund Quarterly: Health and Society* 55:3–24.

Haanes-Olsen, L. 1989. Worldwide Trends and Developments in Social Security, 1985–87. *Social Security Bulletin* 52(2): 14–26.

Haber, L. 1971. Disabling Effects of Chronic Disease and Impairment. *Journal of Chronic Disease* 24(7): 469–487.

Halaby, C. 1986. Worker Attachment and Workplace Authority. *American Sociological Review* 51(October): 634–649.

Halaby, C. and D. Weakliem. 1989. Worker Control and Attachment to the Firm. *American Journal of Sociology* 95(3): 549–591.

Harrrison, B. 1990. The Return of the Big Firms. *Social Policy* 21(1): 7–19.

Harrison, B. and B. Bluestone. 1988. *The Great U-Turn: Corporate Restructuring and the Polarizing of America.* New York: Basic Books.

Haugen, S. and J. Meisenheimer. 1991. U.S. Labor Market Weakened in 1990. *Monthly Labor Review* 114(2): 3–16.

Haveman, R. and B. Wolfe. 1984. The Decline of Male Labor Force Participation: A Comment. *Journal of Political Economy* 92:532–541.

———. 1989. The Economic Well-Being of the Disabled. *Journal of Human Resources* 25(1): 32–54.

Haveman, R., B. Wolfe, and J. Warlick. 1984. Disability Transfers, Early Retirement, and Retrenchment. In *Retirement and Economic Behavior,* edited by H. Aaron and G. Burtless. Washington, D.C.: Brookings Institution.

Hayward, M., W. Grady, M. Hardy, and D. Sommers. 1989. Occupational Influences on Retirement, Disability, and Death. *Demography* 26(3): 393–409.

Hayward M., W. Grady, and S. McLaughlin. 1988. Recent Changes in Mortality and Labor Force Behavior among Older Americans: Consequences for Non-Working Life Expectancy. *Journal of Gerontology* 43(6): S194–199.

Henle, P. and P. Ryscavage. 1980. The Distribution of Earned Income among Men and Women, 1958–1977. *Monthly Labor Review* 103(4): 3–10.

Herz, D. 1990. Worker Displacement in a Period of Rapid Job Expansion: 1983–1987. *Monthly Labor Review* 113(5):21–33.

Hirschhorn, L. 1974. Toward a Political Economy of the Service Society. Institute for Urban and Regional Development Working Paper. Berkeley, California: IURD.

———. 1975. The Social Crisis: The Crisis of Work and Social Services, An Approach to the Grammar of Post-Industrial Revolution. Institute for Urban and Regional Development Working Paper. Berkeley, California: IURD.

———. 1984. *Beyond Mechanization: Work and Technology in a Postindustrial Age.* Cambridge: MIT Press.

———. 1988. *The Workplace Within: Psychodynamics of Organizational Life.* Cambridge: MIT Press.

Homans, G. 1950. *The Human Group.* New York: Harcourt Brace.

Horrigan, M. and J. Markey. 1990. Recent Gains in Women's Earnings: Better Pay or Longer Hours? *Monthly Labor Review* 113(7): 11–17.

Horvath, F. 1987. The Pulse of Economic Change: Displaced Workers of 1981–1985. *Monthly Labor Review* 110(6): 3–12.

Houseman, S. 1991. *Industrial Restructuring with Job Security: The Case of European Steel.* Cambridge: Harvard University Press.

Howards, I., H. Brehm, and S. Nagi. 1980. *Disability: From Social Problem to Federal Program.* New York: Praeger, 1980.

Howe, W. 1990. Labor Market Dynamics and Trends in Male and Female Unemployment. *Monthly Labor Review* 113(11): 3–12.

Howland, M. 1988. Plant Closings and Worker Displacement: The Regional Issues. Kalamazoo, Mich.: Upjohn Institute for Employment Research.

Hurd, M. 1989. The Economic Status of the Elderly. *Science* 244: 659–664.

Iams, H. 1986. Characteristics of the Longest Job for New Disabled Workers: Findings from the New Beneficiary Survey. *Social Security Bulletin* 49(12): 13–18.

Jencks, C., L. Perman, and L. Rainwater. 1988. What Is a Good Job: A New Measure of Labor-Market Success. *American Journal of Sociology* 93(6): 1322–1357.

Johnson, W. and J. Lambrinos. 1985. Wage Discrimination against Handicapped Men and Women. *Journal of Human Resources* 20(2): 264–277.

Jones, S. 1990. Worker Interdependence and Output: The Hawthorne Studies Reevaluated. *American Sociological Review* 55(April): 176–190.

Kalleberg, A. and L. Griffin. 1980. Class, Occupation, and Inequality in Job Rewards. *American Journal of Sociology* 85(4): 731–768.

Kasarda, J. 1989. Urban Industrial Transition and the Underclass. *Annals of the American Academy of Political and Social Science* 501(January): 26–47.

———. 1990. Structural Factors Affecting the Location and Timing of Urban Underclass Growth. *Urban Geography* 11: 234–264.

Kelley, M. 1981. *Labor Supply and Public Policy: A Critical Review.* New York: Academic Press.

———. 1990. New Process Technology, Job Design, and Work Organization: A Contingency Model. *American Sociological Review* 55(April): 191–208.

Kingson, E. 1982. The Health of Very Early Retirees. *Social Security Bulletin* 45(9): 3–9.

Kohn, M. and C. Schooler. 1982. Job Conditions and Personality: A Longitudinal Assessment of Their Reciprocal Effects. *American Journal of Sociology* 87(6): 1257–1286.

Kramer, M. 1980. The Rising Pandemic of Mental Disorders and Associated Chronic Diseases and Disabilities. *Acta Psychiatrica Scandinavica* 62 (supp. 285): 382–396.

Lando, M., R. Cutler, and E. Gamber. 1982. *1978 Survey of Disability and Work: Data Book Preliminary.* Washington, D.C.: GPO.

LaPlante, M. 1988. *Data on Disability from the National Health Interview Survey, 1983–1985.* Washington, D.C.: National Institute for Disability and Rehabilitation Research.

Lawrence, R. 1985. Sectoral Shifts and the Size of the Middle Class. *Brookings Review* 3(4): 3–10.

Lazonick, W. 1990. *Competitive Advantage on the Shop Floor.* Cambridge: Harvard University Press.

Leigh, J. 1985. An Empirical Analysis of Self-Reported Work-Limiting Disability. *Medical Care* 23(4): 310–319.

Leonard, J. 1986. Labor Supply Incentives and Disincentives for Disabled Persons. In *Disability and the Labor Market,* edited by M. Berkowitz and M. Hill. Ithaca, N.Y.: ILR Press.

Levitan, S. and R. Taggart. 1977. *Jobs for the Disabled.* Baltimore: Johns Hopkins University Press.

Levy, F. 1987. *Dollars and Dreams: The Changing American Income Distribution.* New York: Russell Sage Foundation.

Levy, F. and R. Murnane. 1991. Slow Growth Politics. *New York Times,* July 8.

Liang, M., K. Cullen, M. Larson, et al. 1986. Cost-Effectiveness of Total Joint Arthroplasty in Osteoarthritis. *Arthritis and Rheumatism* 29(8): 937–943.

Lichter, D. 1988. Racial Differences in Underemployment in American Cities. *American Journal of Sociology* 93(4): 771–792.

Lincoln, J. and A. Kalleberg. 1990. *Culture, Control, and Commitment: A Study of Work Organization and Work Attitudes in the United States and Japan.* New York: Cambridge University Press.

Linder, M. and G. Houghton. 1990. Comment on Steinmetz and Wright. *American Journal of Sociology* 96(3): 727–735.

Littman, M. 1989. Reasons for Not Working: Poor and Nonpoor Householders. *Monthly Labor Review* 112(8): 16–21.

Lockhart, C. 1989. *Gaining Ground: Tailoring Social Programs to American Values.* Berkeley: University of California Press.

Lozano, B. 1989. *The Invisible Work Force.* New York: Free Press.

Mallet, S. 1975. *The New Working Class.* London: Spokesman Books.

Mansnerus, L. 1991. Boom in Temporary Jobs Eases Lawyer Layoffs. *New York Times,* May 3.

Manton, K. 1982. Changing Concepts of Morbidity and Mortality in the Elderly Population. *Milbank Memorial Fund Quarterly: Health and Society* 60(2): 183–244.

Marmor, T., J. Mashaw, and P. Harvey. 1990. *America's Misunderstood Welfare State: Persistent Myths, Enduring Realities.* New York: Basic Books.

McMahon, P. and J. Tschetter. 1986. The Declining Middle Class: A Further Analysis. *Monthly Labor Review* 109(9): 22–27.

Mellor, E. and W. Parks. 1988. A Year's Work: Labor Force Activity from a Different Perspective. *Monthly Labor Review* 113(9): 13–18.

Mincy, R. 1990. Raising the Minimum Wage: Effects on Family Poverty. *Monthly Labor Review* 113(7): 18–25.

Mincy, R., I. Sawhill, and D. Wolf. 1990. The Underclass: Definition and Measurement. *Science* 248(April 27): 248–253.

Mirkin, B. 1987. Early Retirement as a Labor Force Policy: An International Overview. *Monthly Labor Review* 110(3): 19–33.

Moffitt, R. 1990. The Distribution of Earnings and the Welfare State. In *A Future of Lousy Jobs: The Changing Structure of U.S. Wages,* edited by G. Burtless. Washington, D.C.: Brookings Institution.

Moynihan, D. 1973. *The Politics of a Guaranteed National Income.* New York: Random House.

Murphy, L. 1991. Job Dimensions Associated with Severe Disability due to Cardiovascular Disease. *Journal of Clinical Epidemiology* 44: 155–166.

Murray, C. 1984. *Losing Ground: American Social Policy, 1950–1980.* New York: Basic Books.

Myers, D. 1991. Work After Cessation of Career Job. *Journal of Gerontology* 46(2): S93–102.

Myers, R. 1982. Why Do People Retire from Work Early? *Social Security Bulletin* 45(9): 10–14.

Myles, J. 1988. Postwar Capitalism and the Expansion of Social Security into a Retirement Wage. In *The Politics of Social Policy in the U.S.,* edited by M. Weir, A. Orloff, and T. Skocpol. Princeton: Princeton University Press.

Nagi, S. 1976. An Epidemiology of Disability in the United States. *Milbank Memorial Fund Quarterly: Health and Society* 54(4): 439–468.

Nasar, S. 1991a. Boom in Manufacturing Exports Provides Hope for U.S. Economy: Low Costs and Weak Dollar Contribute to Gains. *New York Times,* April 21.

———. 1991b. Source of Jobs in 80's Fizzles in 90's. *New York Times,* August 24.

Nevitt, M., W. Epstein, M. Masem, et al. 1984. Work Disability before and after Total Hip Arthroplasty. *Arthritis and Rheumatism* 27(4): 410–421.

Noble, D. 1986. *Forces of Production: A Social History of Industrial Automation.* 2nd ed. New York: Oxford Univesity Press.

O'Boyle, T., and C. Hymowitz. 1990. White Collar Blues. *Wall Street Journal.* October 4, A1.

Olshansky, S.J. 1990. Relating the Extension of Life to the Compression of Morbidity: Good News and Bad News. Paper presented at Compression of Morbidity Conference, Pacific Grove, California, March 18–20.

Olshansky, S.J. and A. Ault. 1986. The Fourth Stage of the Epidemiologic Transition: The Age of Delayed Degenerative Diseases. *Milbank Quarterly* 64(3): 355–391.

Osterman, P. 1988. *Employment Futures: Reorganization, Dislocation, and Public Policy.* New York: Oxford University Press.

Parsons, D. 1980. The Decline in Male Labor Force Participation. *Journal of Political Economy* 88(11): 117–134.

———. 1991. Self-Screening in Targeted Public Transfer Programs. *Journal of Political Economy* 99(4): 859–876.

Personick, V. 1989. Industry Output and Employment: A Slower Trend for the Nineties. *Monthly Labor Review* 112(11): 25–41.

Phillips, K. 1990. *The Politics of Rich and Poor: Wealth and the American Electorate in the Reagan Aftermath.* New York: Random House.

Piore, M. and C. Sabel. 1984. *The Second Industrial Divide: Possibilities for Prosperity.* New York: Basic Books.

Plunkert, L. 1990. The 1980's: A Decade of Job Growth and Industry Shifts. *Monthly Labor Review* 113(9): 3–16.

Polivka, A. and T. Nardone. 1989. On The Definition of Contingent Work. *Monthly Labor Review* 112(12): 9–16.

Preston, S. 1984. Children and the Elderly: Divergent Paths for America's Dependent Population. *Demography* 21(4): 435–457.

Ransom, R. and R. Sutch. 1988. The Decline of Retirement in the Years Before Social Security: U.S. Retirement Patterns, 1870–1940. In *Issues in Contemporary Retirement* edited by R. Ricardo-Campbell and E. Lazear. Stanford, Calif.: Hoover Institution Press.

Reisine, S., K. Grady, C. Goodenow, and J. Fifield. 1989. Work Disability among Women with Rheumatoid Arthritis. *Arthritis and Rheumatism* 32: 538–543.

Reskin, B. and P. Roos. 1990. *Job Queues, Gender Queues: Explaining Women's Inroads into Male Occupations.* Philadelphia: Temple University Press.

Rice, D. and M. LaPlante. 1988. Chronic Illness, Disability, and Increasing Longevity. In *The Economics and Ethics of Long Term Care,* edited by S. Sullivan, and M. Lewin. Washington, D.C.: American Enterprise Institute for Public Policy Research.

Rivlin, A. and J. Wiener. 1988. *Caring for the Disabled Elderly.* Washington, D.C.: Brookings Institution.

Rosenthal, N. 1985. The Shrinking Middle Class: Myth or Reality? *Monthly Labor Review* 108(3): 3–10.

———. 1989. More than Wages at Issue in Job Quality Debate. *Monthly Labor Review* 112(12): 4–18.

Rothschild, J. and J. Whitt. 1986. *The Cooperative Workplace: Potentials and Dilemmas of Organizational Democracy and Participation.* New York: Cambridge University Press.

Ryscavage, P. and P. Henle. 1990. Earnings Inequality Accelerates in the 1980's. *Monthly Labor Review* 113(12): 3–16.

Schlaifer, R. 1980. The Relay Assembly Test Room: An Alternative Statistical Interpretation. *American Sociological Review* 45: 995–1005.

Schorr, L. and D. Schorr. 1988. *Within Our Reach: Breaking the Cycle of Disadvantage.* New York: Doubleday.

Schumpeter J. [1942] 1950. *Capitalism, Socialism, and Democracy.* New York: Harper.

Scotch, R. 1984. *From Good Will to Civil Rights: Transforming Federal Disability Policy.* Philadelphia: Temple University Press.

Seitchick, A. and J. Zornitsky. 1989. From One Job to the Next: Worker Adjustment in a Changing Labor Market. Kalamazoo, Mich.: Upjohn Institute for Employment Research.

Shaiken, H., S. Herzenberg, and S. Kuhn. 1986. The Work Process under More Flexible Production. *Industrial Relations* 25(2): 167–183.

Shank, S. 1986. Preferred Hours of Work and Corresponding Earnings. *Monthly Labor Review* 109(11): 40–47.

Sheppard, H. and S. Rix. 1979. *The Graying of Working America.* New York: Free Press.

Sherman, S. 1985. Reported Reasons Retired Workers Left Their Last Job: Findings from the New Beneficiary Survey. *Social Security Bulletin* 48(3): 22–30.

Silvestri, G. and J. Lukasiewicz. 1989. Projections of Occupational Employment, 1988–2000. *Monthly Labor Review* 112(11):42–65.

Sing, B. 1990. Protect Your Insurance When You Change Jobs. *Los Angeles Times,* April 22.

Solow, R. 1957. Technical Change and the Aggregate Production Function. Review of Economics and Statistics 39 (August): 312–320.

Spenner, K. 1979. Temporal Changes in Work Content. *American Sociological Review* 44(December): 968–975.

Starr, P. 1982. *The Social Transformation of American Medicine.* New York: Basic Books.

Stein, B. 1980. *Social Security and Pensions in Transition.* New York: Free Press.

Steinmetz, G. and E. Wright. 1989. The Rise and Fall of the Petty Bourgeoisie: Changing Patterns of Self-Employment in the Postwar United States. *American Journal of Sociology* 94(5): 973–1018.

Stern, S. 1989. Measuring the Effect of Disability on Labor Force Participation. *Journal of Human Resources* 24(3): 361–395.

Stevens, B. 1988. Blurring the Boundaries: How the Federal Government Has Influenced the Welfare Benefits in the Private Sector. In *The Politics of Social Policy in the U.S.,* edited by M. Weir, A. Orloff, and T. Skocpol. Princeton: Princeton University Press.

Stevens, R. 1971. *American Medicine and the Public Interest.* New Haven: Yale University Press.

Stockman, D. 1986. *The Triumph of Politics: How the Reagan Revolution Failed.* New York: Harper and Row.

Stolnitz, G. 1964. The Demographic Transition: From High to Low Birth Rates and Death Rates. In *Population: The Vital Revolution,* edited by R. Freedman. New York: Anchor, 1964.

Stone, D. 1984. *The Disabled State.* Philadelphia: Temple University Press.

Swaim, P. and M. Podgursky. 1989. Do More Educated Workers Fare Better Following Job Displacement? *Monthly Labor Review* 112(8): 43–46.

Taylor, F. [1911] 1967. *The Principles of Scientific Management.* Reprint, New York: Norton.

Touraine, A. 1971. *The Post-Industrial Society.* New York: Random House.

Tuma, N. and G. Sandefur. 1988. Trends in the Labor Force Activity of the Elderly in the United States, 1940–1980. In *Issues in Contemporary Retirement,* edited by R. Ricardo-Campbell and E. Lazear. Stanford, Calif.: Hoover Institution Press.

Uchitelle, L. 1991a. Why Older Men Keep on Working. *New York Times,* April 23.

———. 1991b. A Growing Drag From Services. *New York Times,* September 24.

———. 1991c. Insurance Linked to Jobs: System Showing Its Age. *New York Times,* May 1.

U.S. Bureau of the Census. 1972. *Statistical Abstract of the United States, 1972.* Washington, D.C.: GPO.

———. 1975. *Statistical Abstract of the United States, 1975.* Washington, D.C.: GPO.

———. 1976. *Historical Statistics of the United States: Colonial Times to 1970.* Washington, D.C.: GPO.

———. 1977. Statistical Abstract of the United States, 1977. Washington, D.C.: GPO.

———. 1981. *Statistical Abstract of the United States, 1981.* Washington, D.C.: GPO.

———. 1983a. *Labor Force Status and Other Characteristics of Persons with a Work Disability.* Current Population Reports, series P-23, no. 127. Washington, D.C.: GPO.

———. 1983b. *Statistical Abstract of the United States, 1982–1983.* Washington, D.C.: GPO.

———. 1984. *Statistical Abstract of the United States, 1984.* Washington, D.C.: GPO.

———. 1984a. *Demographic Socioeconomic Aspects of Aging in the United States.* Current Population Reports, series P-23, no. 138. Washington, D.C.: GPO.

———. 1985. *Statistical Abstract of the United States, 1985.* Washington, D.C.: GPO.

———. 1986. *Statistical Abstract of the United States, 1986.* Washington, D.C.: GPO.

———. 1987. *Statistical Abstract of the United States, 1987.* Washington, D.C.: GPO.

———. 1988. *Statistical Abstract of the United States, 1988.* Washington, D.C.: GPO.

———. 1989a. *Statistical Abstract of the United States, 1989.* Washington, D.C.: GPO.

———. 1989b. *Labor Force Status and Other Characteristics of Persons with a Work Disability.* Current Population Reports, series P-23, no. 160. Washington, D.C.: GPO.

———. 1989c. *Projections of the Population of the United States, by Age, Sex, and Race, 1988 to 2080.* Current Population Reports, series P-25, no. 1018. Washington, D.C.: GPO.

———. 1990. *Statistical Abstract of the United States, 1990.* Washington, D.C.: GPO.

U.S. Congress. House. Select Committee on Aging. 1984a. *Social Security*

Disability Review: A Costly Constitutional Crisis. 98th Congress, 2nd. sess.

———. Senate. Special Committee on Aging. 1984b. *Social Security Disability Reviews: The Human Costs.* 98th Congress, 2nd. sess.

U.S. Department of Health and Human Services. 1982. *Social Security Bulletin* 45(8): 3–14.

———. 1985a. *Health: United States, 1985.* Washington, D.C.: GPO.

———. 1985b. *Social Security Bulletin. Annual Statistical Supplement, 1984/1985.*

———. 1986a. *Social Security Bulletin. Annual Statistical Supplement, 1986.*

———. 1986b. *Social Security Bulletin* 49(7): 34–37.

———. 1987. *Social Security Bulletin. Annual Statistical Supplement , 1987.*

———. 1989a. Advance Report of Final Mortality Statistics, 1987. *Monthly Vital Statistics* 38(5): supp. table 2.

———. 1989b. *Social Security Bulletin, Annual Statistical Supplement, 1989.*

———. 1990a. *Social Security Bulletin* 53(11): 51,71–72.

———. 1990b. *Social Security Bulletin, Annual Statistical Supplement, 1990.*

U.S. Department of Labor. 1961. *Employment and Earnings Report.* Washington, D.C.: GPO.

———. 1971. *Employment and Earnings Report.* Washington, D.C.: GPO.

———. 1981. *Employment and Earnings Report.* Washington, D.C.: GPO.

———. 1983. *Monthly Labor Review* 106(6): 86–88.

———. 1984. *Monthly Labor Review* 107(6): 99–101.

———. 1985a. *Monthly Labor Review* 108(6): 91–93.

———. 1985b. *Handbook of Labor Statistics.* Washington, D.C.: GPO.

———. 1986a. *Monthly Labor Review* 109(6): 78–80.

———. 1986b. *Employment and Earnings Report.* Washington, D.C.: GPO.

———. 1987. *Monthly Labor Review* 110(5): 86–88.

———. 1988a. *Employment and Earnings Report.* Washington, D.C.: GPO.

———. 1988b. *Labor Force Statistics Derived from the Current Population Survey, 1948–1987.* Washington, D.C.: GPO.

———. 1988c. *Monthly Labor Review* 111(10): 39–41.

———. 1990a. *Monthly Labor Review* 113(5): 84–87, 91–94.

———. 1990b. *Monthly Labor Review* 113(10): 39–41.

———. 1991a. *Monthly Labor Review* 114(1): 88.

———. 1991b. *Monthly Labor Review* 114(2): 96.

———. 1991c. *Monthly Labor Review* 114(6): 70, 99.

Verbrugge, L. 1984. Longer Life but Worsening Health? Trends in Health and Mortality of Middle-Aged and Older Persons. *Milbank Quarterly* 62(3): 475–519.

⸺. 1989. Recent, Present, and Future Health of American Adults. *Annual Review of Public Health* 10:333–361.

⸺. 1990. The Iceberg of Disability. In *The Legacy of Longevity* edited by S. Stahl. Newbury Park, Calif.: Sage.

Wardwell, W. 1979. Critique of a Recent Professional Put-Down of the Hawthorne Research. *American Sociological Review* 44: 858–861.

Watson, S. 1990. Disability Management: Implications for Public and Private Policies. Paper presented at National Council on Disability Conference on Writing National Policy on Work Disability, Washington, D.C., November 29.

Weakliem, D. 1990. Relative Wages and the Radical Theory of Economic Segmentation. *American Sociological Review* 55(August): 574–590.

Weinberger, M, J. Darnell, W. Tierney, B. Martz, S. Hiner, et al. 1986. Self-Rated Health as a Predictor of Hospital Admissions and Nursing Home Placement in Elderly Public Housing Tenants. *American Journal of Public Health* 76:457–459.

Weinstein, J. 1968. *The Corporate Ideal and the Liberal State.* Boston: Beacon Press.

Wiebe, R. 1967. *The Search for Order, 1877–1920.* Boston: Hill and Wang.

Wilson R, and T. Drury. 1984. Interpreting Trends in Illness and Disability: Health Statistics and Health Status. *Annual Review of Public Health* 5: 83–106.

Wilson, W. 1987. *The Truly Disadvantaged: The Inner City, the Underclass, and Public Policy.* Chicago: University of Chicago Press.

⸺. 1991. Studying Inner-City Social Dislocations: The Challenge of Public Agenda Research. *American Sociological Review* 56(February): 1–14.

Wolfe, B. and R. Haveman. 1990. Trends in the Prevalence of Work Disability from 1962 to 1984, and Their Correlates. *Milbank Quarterly* 68(1): 53–80.

Wright, E. and B. Martin. 1987. The Transformation of the American Class Structure, 1960–1980. *American Journal of Sociology* 93(1): 1–29.

Wright, E. and J. Singleman. 1982. Proletarianization in the American Class Structure. In *Marxist Inquiries,* edited by M. Buroway and T. Skocpol. Special issue of *American Journal of Sociology* 88(supp.): 176–209.

Ycas, M. 1988. Are the Eighties Different? Continuity and Change in the Health of Older Persons. In *Proceedings of the 1987 Public Health Conference on Records and Statistics.* Department of Health and Human Serices Publication no. 88–1214. Washington, D.C.: GPO.

Yelin, E. 1986. The Myth of Malingering: Why Individuals Withdraw from Work in the Presence of Illness. *Milbank Quarterly* 64(4): 622–650.

———. 1989. Displaced Concern: The Social Context of the Work Disability Problem. *Milbank Quarterly* 67 (supp. 2, part 1), 114–166.

———. 1991. The Recent History and Immediate Future of Employment among Persons with Disabilities. In *From Policy to Practice: Implementing the Americans with Disabilities Act,* edited by J. West. New York: Milbank Memorial Fund.

Yelin, E., R. Greenblatt, H. Hollander, and J. McMaster. 1991. The Impact of HIV-Related Illness on Employment. *American Journal of Public Health* 81(1): 79–84.

Yelin, E., C. Henke, and W. Epstein. 1986. Work Disability among Persons with Musculoskeletal Conditions. *Arthritis and Rheumatism* 29: 1322–1333.

———. 1987. The Work Dynamics of the Person with Rheumatoid Arthritis. *Arthritis and Rheumatism* 30: 507–512.

Yelin, E. and P. Katz. 1990. Transitions in Health Status among Community-Dwelling Elderly People with Arthritis. *Arthritis and Rheumatism* 33: 1205–1215.

———. 1991. Labor Force Participation among Persons with Arthritis, 1970–1987: National Estimates Derived from a Series of Cross-Sections. *Arthritis and Rheumatism* 34(11): 1361–1370.

Yelin, E., R. Meenan, M. Nevitt, and W. Epstein. 1980. Work Disability in Rheumatoid Arthritis: Effects of Disease, Social, and Work Factors. *Annals of Internal Medicine* 93: 551–556.

Yelin, E., M. Nevitt, and W. Epstein. 1980. Toward an Epidemiology of Work Disability. *Milbank Memorial Fund Quarterly: Health and Society* 58(3): 386–415.

Zuboff, S. 1988. *In the Age of the Smart Machine: The Future of Work and Power.* New York: Basic Books.

Author Index

Subject Index

(Page numbers in italics indicate material in tables or figures.)